The

CIVIL WAR

1860–1865

The CIVIL WAR

1860–1865

Christopher Collier
James Lincoln Collier

BENCHMARK BOOKS

MARSHALL CAVENDISH
NEW YORK

ACKNOWLEDGMENT: The authors wish to thank Professor David Blight of Amherst College for his careful reading of the text of this volume of The Drama of American History and his thoughtful and useful comments. The work has been much improved by Professor Blight's notes. The authors are deeply in his debt, but of course, assume full responsibility for the substance of the work, including any errors that may appear.

Photo research by James Lincoln Collier
COVER PHOTO: © Corbis-Bettman
PICTURE CREDITS: The photographs in this book are used by permission and through the courtesy of :
Corbis-Bettmann: 10, 15, 17, 20, 22, 33, 38, 48, 50, 51, 55, 57, 60, 62, 68, 72, 75, 76, 80, 83, 86.
Abby Aldrich Rockefeller Folk Art Center: 12 (top). Library of Congress: 12 (bottom), 26 (top),
26 (bottom), 28, 29, 42, 45 (top), 45 (bottom), 52, 66, 74.

Benchmark Books
Marshal Cavendish Corporation
99 White Plains Road
Tarrytown, New York, 10591-9001

@2000 Christopher Collier and James Lincoln Collier

Library of Congress Cataloging-in-Publication Data

Collier, Christopher, (date)
The Civil War, 1860–1865 / Christopher Collier, James Lincoln Collier.
p.   cm. -- (Drama of American history)
Includes bibliographical references and index.
Summary: Examines the people and events involved in bloody war that pitted the
Northern states against those that seceded to form the Confederacy.
ISBN 0-7614-0818-5 (lib. bdg.)
1. United States--History--Civil War, 1861–1865--Juvenile literature.
[1. United States--History--Civil War, 1861–1865.]
I. Collier, James Lincoln, (date). II. Title. III. Series: Collier, Christopher, (date)
Drama of American history.
E468.C72 2000
973.7--dc21

97-49178
CIP
AC

Printed in Italy

1 3 5 6 4 2

CONTENTS

Over many years of both teaching and writing for students at all levels, from grammar school to graduate school, it has been borne in on us that many, if not most, American history textbooks suffer from trying to include everything of any moment in the history of the nation. Students become lost in a swamp of factual information, and as a consequence lose track of how those facts fit together and why they are significant and relevant to the world today.

In this series, our effort has been to strip the vast amount of available detail down to a central core. Our aim is to draw in bold strokes, providing enough information, but no more than is necessary, to bring out the basic themes of the American story, and what they mean to us now. We believe that it is surely more important for students to grasp the underlying concepts and ideas that emerge from the movement of history, than to memorize an array of facts and figures.

The difference between this series and many standard texts lies in what has been left out. We are convinced that students will better remember the important themes if they are not buried under a heap of names, dates, and places.

In this sense, our primary goal is what might be called citizenship education. We think it is critically important for America as a nation and Americans as individuals to understand the origins and workings of the public institutions that are central to American society. We have asked ourselves again and again what is most important for citizens of our democracy to know so they can most effectively make the system work for them and the nation. For this reason, we have focused on political and institutional history, leaving social and cultural history less well developed.

This series is divided into volumes that move chronologically through the American story. Each is built around a single topic, such as the Pilgrims, the Constitutional Convention, or immigration. Each volume has been written so that it can stand alone, for students who wish to research a given topic. As a consequence, in many cases material from previous volumes is repeated, usually in abbreviated form, to set the topic in its historical context. That is to say, students of the Constitutional Convention must be given some idea of relations with England, and why the Revolution was fought, even though the material was covered in detail in a previous volume. Readers should find that each volume tells an entire story that can be read with or without reference to other volumes.

Despite our belief that it is of the first importance to outline sharply basic concepts and generalizations, we have not neglected the great dramas of American history. The stories that will hold the attention of students are here, and we believe they will help the concepts they illustrate to stick in their minds. We think, for example, that knowing of Abraham Baldwin's brave and dramatic decision to vote with the small states at the Constitutional Convention will bring alive the Connecticut Compromise, out of which grew the American Senate.

Each of these volumes has been read by esteemed specialists in its particular topic; we have benefited from their comments.

CHAPTER I

The Coming of the War

The Civil War was one of the greatest dramas in American history, a story so filled with blood, glory, terror, and triumph that it has been the subject of over fifty thousand serious books in English. Not just Americans, but people all around the world have been fascinated by it. The idea of brother against brother has always been compelling. The Civil War split Americans, in many cases dividing families so that brothers, fathers, and sons fought on opposite sides: Senator John Crittenden of Kentucky had one son a general in the Confederate army, another a general in the Union army.

The question that hovers like a ghost over any discussion of the Civil War is this: Did it really have to be fought? Was all that bloodshed, bringing death to 620,000 Americans, unavoidable? To understand why this conflict happened, we need to step back a little in time and watch the events leading up to it unfold.

At the Convention of 1787, when the U.S. Constitution was written, it became clear that there were natural differences between the Northern and Southern parts of the nation. Their climates were different, leading to differing kinds of farming and lifestyles. The South was agricultural,

The beginning and the end: Edmund Ruffin, of the Palmetto Guards of South Carolina, fired the first shot at Fort Sumter on April 14, 1861. He shot himself on June 15, 1865, when it became clear that the South would lose the war, because he was unwilling to live under the United States government.

depending for almost all of its income on growing tobacco, rice, sugar, and, in the nineteenth century, especially cotton. The North, too, had its farms, but it also had a growing industry, a merchant fleet, a fishing trade; banks and export companies in New York and Philadelphia controlled the nation's commerce. As a consequence, the South was dependent on Northern export merchants and Northern ships to move its cotton and tobacco to markets, as well as on Northern banks for financing.

Most particularly, the South had slavery, the North very little of it. And at the Constitutional Convention of 1787 James Madison, a Southerner, pointed out that slavery was the key difference between the regions. Many Northern delegates to the Convention were opposed to slavery, and favored limiting it in one way or another in hopes that it would eventually die out. But probably the majority of Northerners were indifferent to it. While there were Southerners such as George Washington and Thomas Jefferson who found slavery distasteful, most plantation owners felt it essential to them, some as a necessary evil, but others as good for both white Americans and the enslaved Africans. It was clear to the Northern delegates in 1787 that most Southern states would not join a Union bent on ending slavery. To almost everybody at the Convention it was more important to form a workable Union than battle over slavery, and the Constitution as finally written guaranteed slavery in the states where it existed—which in 1787 was all of them except Massachusetts. But these differences in attitudes and reliance on slave labor were fraught with the potential for future rivalry—which would lead ultimately to deadly antagonisms.

Over the decades after the end of the Revolutionary War in 1783, Northerners step-by-step outlawed slavery in their own states. Hatred of slavery kept growing in the North, and by 1820 there was considerable opinion against it there. Partly this was out of moral or religious conviction, partly because many Northerners considered blacks inferior and did not want them around, free or slave. Northerners recognized that there was little they could do to eliminate slavery in the old Southern states; but out to the west there was a vast amount of land that was not in any state, but belonged to the whole American people. This great territory would eventually have to be cut into states, and many Northerners were determined that slavery should not be permitted there. As a result, bitter political battles were fought over slavery in new states and territories, like Missouri and California. Leading politicians cared enough about the Union, however, to work out compromises. But during the debate over slavery in the Kansas and Nebraska territories in 1856, actual warfare, with about two hundred deaths, flamed up. Eventually a compromise was worked out here, too, but it left both sides feeling angry with the result. (For more detail on the events leading up to the Civil War see the volume in this series called *Slavery and the Coming of the Civil War*.) Neither side was in a mood for further compromises.

The election of 1860 applied the match to the tinder. The Democrats were the strongest political party, but the party was split down the middle between Southerners who wanted slavery guaranteed and protected in all new states and territories; and Northerners who would let climate and soil determine the status of slavery in the West. Southern and

North and South differed in many ways. Above, a scene from Montgomery County, Virginia, showing a typical plantation house, a tobacco barn in the foreground, and travelers in a coach. Most Southerners lived in rural circumstances like this. This sketch was drawn by an amateur artist of the day, Lewis Miller. At left, New England whalers closing in on their prey. The North had extensive fleets, and for the time, large-scale manufactures.

Northern Democrats each nominated their own candidate for president. Thus divided, they could not win, and the presidency fell to the candidate of the new Republican Party, a man who had recently become well known himself, Abraham Lincoln.

Lincoln disliked slavery, but the Constitution protected it in the states where it already existed, and any attempt to alter that arrangement would certainly cause Southern states to secede from the United States. However, he did not want to see slavery spread to territories that would in time become new states. Southerners concluded that they now had a president who was dead set against slavery, and on December 20, 1860, South Carolina seceded from the Union. Within the next six weeks Georgia, Mississippi, Alabama, Louisiana, Texas, and Florida also seceded, and these seven states started to form their own nation.

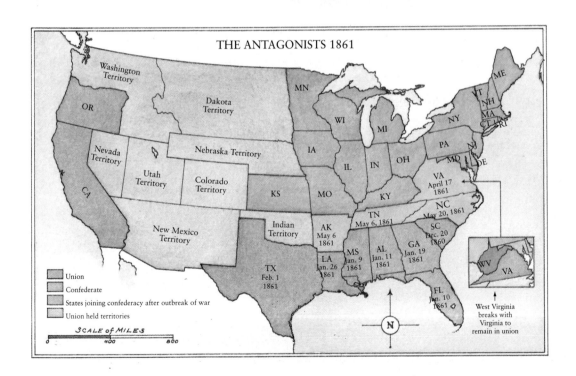

THE ANTAGONISTS 1861

Union
Confederate
States joining confederacy after outbreak of war
Union held territories

SCALE of MILES
0   400   800

West Virginia breaks with Virginia to remain in union

Is there any way this chain of events could have been halted? This is a question historians have puzzled over for more than a hundred years. Many compromises were suggested; but in the end, animosity between North and South had built to the point where a great many people on both sides refused to compromise. Abraham Lincoln, in a famous speech, said that the United States could not exist half free and half slave. "A house divided against itself cannot stand," he said. And he may well have been right. Whereas economic and political interests can usually be compromised, moral questions cannot. Emotions for and against slavery were too strong to exist side-by-side in the same nation.

Abraham Lincoln has been called the man nobody knows. This is surprising, because probably no American has been written about so much. We know his hat size, how tall he was. We have many photographs of him, a mask of his face and hands, in addition to many portraits. And yet, much of what we think we know about him is misleading. For example, almost all of the photographs of him, as well as his image on our pennies and five-dollar bills, show a stern, unsmiling face. We must realize, however, that in the days before high-speed cameras, people had to pose for minutes while the image was caught on film. A photographer could not catch a face in action as we can today. People who knew Lincoln said his face was very mobile, always in motion, and that he had a quick smile and a ready laugh.

He was a striking man to look at—almost six-foot-four, skinny with very long legs. He had been raised as a rough country youth doing hard farm work, and in later life he remained extremely strong. He was not afraid of a fight, and could easily beat most men, as he did a few times when forced to.

He was a man who loved to tell stories—anecdotes about people he had known, about fellow politicians. Often he used such stories to put aside questions people asked of him. He could tell a good joke, too. He was good company, and enjoyed sitting around with people and talking.

Abraham Lincoln was clean shaven even as he started his campaign for the presidency, but grew a beard when a little girl told him that he would look better with one.

He never talked much about his childhood and family, however.

What matters to us most about Abraham Lincoln is his intelligence. He had an extraordinary ability to cut to the heart of a problem. He could see what was at the bottom of a political question or hot issue. He was realistic when faced with hard decisions, as he was almost daily. He could see what the real choices were, and, holding out not for impossible goals, would take what he could get.

He was, furthermore, extremely good at handling people. He would express his ideas clearly and with humor, in such a way that they seemed reasonable to others. But when he could not persuade people to his position, he was not afraid to use his power. Once, at a cabinet meeting all the others voted against what Lincoln wanted. He announced that the vote was nine nays, one aye—and the ayes have it. Abraham Lincoln is considered to be one of the greatest of all Americans, and he was, because of the clarity of his understanding and his great skill in defining issues and articulating them in the most expressive and appealing language. Above all was his brilliance in managing other people.

Critically important, of course, was Lincoln's opinion of slavery. Today it is difficult to understand how anyone, especially a president, could be in favor of slavery. Yet in the mid-nineteenth century there were millions of Americans, not only in the South, who felt that slavery was ordained by God, sanctioned by the Bible, and accepted by tradition. Many people even believed that American slavery was good for Africans because it Christianized and "civilized" them. It could not be taken for granted that presidents were necessarily opposed to slavery, as many had not been; indeed a half dozen or more had owned slaves themselves.

Lincoln had always, so he said, hated slavery. He once wrote a friend about seeing some slaves shackled in irons while he was on a boat trip. "The sight was a continual torment to me," he said.

Yet he knew he had to compromise with Southern politicians if he was to keep the nation intact. Like many Americans, Lincoln believed that slavery would die out if it were not allowed to spread. That meant keeping it out of new states as much as possible. He said, "We should never knowingly lend ourselves directly or indirectly to prevent slavery from dying a natural death—[we should not] find new places for it to live in, when it can no longer exist in the old." He wanted, he said, to give the pioneers in the western territories "a clean bed with no snakes in it."

But as strongly as Abraham Lincoln opposed the spread of slavery, he was even more strongly determined to keep the United States from splitting up. He insisted that under the Constitution "no state, upon its own mere motion, can lawfully get out of the Union." His oath of office required him to "preserve, protect, and defend," the government and to see "that the laws of the Union be faithfully executed in all the States."

As the law then stood, Lincoln would not take office until March 1861, four months after the election. The president until then would be the Democrat James Buchanan, who, for various reasons, had not been nominated for a second term. Buchanan was a decent and intelligent man, a Pennsylvanian who disliked slavery but sympathized with the Southern point of view, which made him a "doughface," a Northern man with Southern principles. He was eager for a compromise that might save the Union. But he could find no solution. The immediate problem was that Southern states were taking over Federal post offices, customs houses, army depots, forts, navy yards wherever they could within their own boundaries; and Buchanan said he could find no clause in the Constitution that permitted the president to do anything about it.

By the time of Lincoln's inauguration seven Southern states had seceded, and it was clear that war was in the offing. Congressmen and other politicians began making frantic efforts to find compromises acceptable to both sides. Large numbers of white Southerners, especially those in the inland mountainous areas where few owned slaves and many hated the plantation aristocrats who controlled state politics, did not wish to leave the Union. They would remain loyal to the United States throughout the war and help reorganize their states when it was over. But the men in the new Confederate government had already decided that the

President James Buchanan was in office when the Southern states began to secede. He was unable to decide what to do, and let matters drift until Lincoln took over.

South would be better off outside the Union, and were not looking for compromises. Buchanan was urged to reinforce Federal army and navy posts, and hold them, but as a lame-duck president, soon to leave office, he would not take action. This, then, was the situation when Lincoln took office in March 1861. Lincoln was made of stronger metal than Buchanan.

One Federal strong point the Confederates did not take over immediately was Fort Sumter, on a tiny island in Charleston Harbor. It was occupied by a small force of United States troops under the command of Major Robert Anderson. Lincoln, too, wanted to avoid a war; but he was

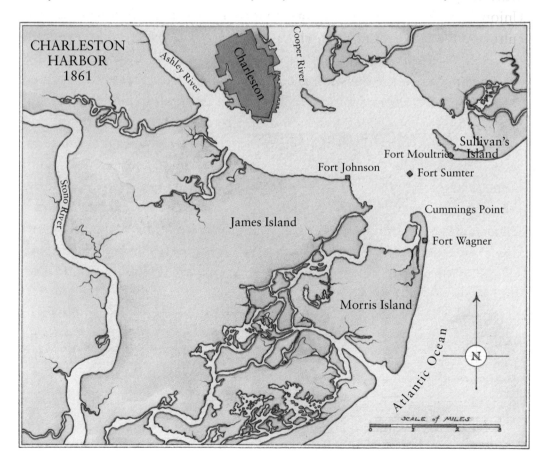

not prepared to give up Fort Sumter, for he had sworn to "preserve, protect, and defend" the United States. Fearing that the Southern forces would starve Major Anderson out, Lincoln announced that he would send provisions, but no reinforcements or arms if South Carolina would let the provision ship through. However, the new Confederate government was determined to take the fort, and on April 12, 1861, at 4:30 in the morning, guns from Charleston began to fire on Fort Sumter. Thirty-four hours later Anderson was forced to surrender. The war was on.

Now there arises another of the tantalizing questions about the Civil War: Why was it so important to Lincoln, and many others, to keep the Union intact? As the nation was divided by so many factors—slavery, culture, climate, and more—why wouldn't it be better to let the two halves exist side-by-side as separate nations? What harm would it do?

The answer to the question is complex. The United States was formed as great experiment in democracy. In Lincoln's day, almost everywhere on earth ordinary human beings were ruled by kings, queens, princes, and noblemen who often had absolute power over their subjects. A great many people believed it had to be that way—that ordinary men and women were not able to govern themselves. In setting up their own government, the people of the newly independent United States had done something so striking as to seem around the world almost miraculous. The Founding Fathers of 1776 and 1787 were sure that they were in the vanguard of the world, blazing a trail that other nations would follow. And in this they were right.

Many Americans, thus, had an almost mystic belief in the importance of the United States. Today, when democracy is common, although by no means universal, we cannot see how unusual it was in Abraham Lincoln's day. He felt that the worst possible thing to happen would be for the great American experiment in democracy to fail. And it worried him deeply that the division of the Union would lead to a general collapse of the whole nation. Even at that moment France was attempting to take

Fort Sumter shortly after the Union surrendered it. Note the state flag flying. The bombardment of Sumter caused considerable damage, but no fatalities, unlike the remainder of the war, in which hundreds of thousands were killed.

over Mexico: Would it not then push outward into Texas and the Southwest, which a weak Confederacy might find hard to defend? England, which needed Southern cotton for its textile mills, might then begin to prey on the Southern states. The dangers were many, and they seemed to many Americans real. If the United States went down, taking with it the hard-won democracy, it would be a tragedy for all mankind. So Lincoln would fight. And so, too, would millions of American men and boys.

And in the four bloody years that followed, one team of historians writes, "American society underwent a social revolution of mammoth proportions. The government was transformed, social classes rearranged, citizenship redefined, billions of dollars of property expropriated without compensation, and the relations of free labor forcibly substituted for those of slavery."

CHAPTER II

The Terrible War Begins

On February 8, 1861, delegates from Alabama, Florida, Mississippi, Louisiana, Texas, South Carolina, and Georgia met at Montgomery, Alabama, and formed the Confederate States of America. They drew up a Constitution that was much like the Constitution of the United States, except that it officially authorized slavery, and said expressly that it was a compact of "sovereign states." The point of terms like *confederation* and *sovereign states* was to make clear something Southern politicians had been insisting upon for a generation or more: States should have the right to nullify congressional legislation if they chose. This idea would cause Southerners problems in fighting the war.

The delegates then elected as president Jefferson Davis, until then a U.S. senator from Mississippi. (Davis was elected again in regular elections in November 1861 after Virginia, North Carolina, Tennessee, and Arkansas had joined the Confederacy.) Many historians have noted the contrast between Abraham Lincoln and Jefferson Davis. Where Lincoln was tolerant and humorous, Davis was thin skinned and quick to lash out at people who disagreed with him. Where Lincoln was usually able to persuade people to his ideas, and compromise when necessary, Davis always fought to have his own way. Where Lincoln was modest about his gifts, Davis, a West Point graduate, thought he was a genius who knew better than his own generals how to fight the war.

Jefferson Davis, nonetheless, was an honest, intelligent, high-minded man who had distinguished himself in many ways. Born into an ordinary family, he became an officer in the United States Army, and eventually gained a celebrated, if small, victory in the Mexican War. A war hero in the eyes of many, he was elected to Congress, then the Senate, and finally was chosen to be secretary of war by President Franklin Pierce in 1853.

Unfortunately for Davis, there was that clause about "sovereign states" in the Confederate Constitution. States that did not want to cooperate with the Confederate government could use the clause as an excuse not to: Davis spent much of the war futilely trying to argue his own countrymen into supplying their army with men, arms, and money. Had Jefferson Davis been as good a politician as Lincoln, who was clear-thinking and persuasive, he

Jefferson Davis was an intelligent, honorable man, devoted to his beloved South. But he was also rigid and certain of his opinions, and lacked Lincoln's ability to bring people over to his way of thinking.

might have been better able to get his own people to do what was necessary to win. But after some early success in bringing together the proud and stubborn Southern state politicians, Davis tended toward arrogance and stubbornness himself. He assumed that he was a better military leader than most of his generals, and frequently gave them misguided orders. Unquestionably, differences in personality between Lincoln and Davis were important factors in the Union triumph. In Davis's defense, it must be said that people like Abraham Lincoln are rare indeed.

The war began with much confidence and martial spirit on both sides. Americans had not fought a serious war on their home soil for three generations: They knew only from books and legends of the glories of Bunker Hill and Yorktown; they did not remember the heaps of American bodies lying on the fields at Brandywine and Germantown.

Paradoxically, both sides thought they were fighting for constitutional rights. Southerners had long believed that the more populous and wealthier North was trying to "enslave" it, as some said. Slavery was protected by the Constitution, and hostile efforts to restrict it by Northerners violated the Constitution. Slaves were property, Southerners pointed out, and the Fifth Amendment, with other constitutional clauses, protected everyone's property no matter where they took it. Northerners felt they were simply trying to prevent the South from violating the Constitution by breaking up the Union. Southerners were trying to declare their own independence and compared themselves to their patriotic grandfathers who had fought to free America from England. Emotions ran high: Both sides thought they were morally and constitutionally in the right. How, therefore, could they lose? Southerners were sure that any one of their men was a match for a dozen Yankees. Both sides, in any case, believed that it would be a short war, over in a few weeks. Lincoln was so hopeful of an early victory that, at first, he called for Northern enlistments of only ninety days. But he greatly overestimated the strength of loyalty to the Union among Southerners.

U.S. Naval officers in 1864 on the deck of the Susquehanna, *one of the vessels stationed off the Southern coast as part of the blockade. While many Southern ships slipped through the blockade, it was effective enough to keep the South from getting many of the supplies it needed.*

The South countered the blockade with low-slung steam vessels burning hard coal, which gave off less telltale smoke than soft coal. This blockade-runner was called Teaser.

sand trips were made through the blockade during the four years of the war, compared with twenty thousand in the four years just before the war. Only a half million bales of cotton were shipped out of the South during the war, as compared with ten million over a similar period before the war. No question about it: The blockade had a major effect on the South's ability to fight.

But the blockade alone could not win the war. Lincoln knew that the Northern armies would have to drive into the South and defeat the Confederate armies. So did ordinary citizens, and during the first weeks after Fort Sumter, Northern newspapers and politicians kept up a drumfire of demands that Lincoln *do* something—most especially drive on the Confederate capital at Richmond, Virginia, only a little over a hundred miles to the south, and bring down the Confederacy at one stroke.

It quickly became clear to Lincoln that General Scott had to be replaced. The seventy-five-year-old Scott had fought valiantly in the War of 1812, and had been the hero of the Mexican War. His Anaconda idea would prove to be a good one, but he was slow to get going.

Finally in mid-July Northern troops, under the command of General Irvin McDowell, began to move toward the Confederate army, which had gathered around the little town of Manassas, Virginia, about thirty miles southwest of Washington. Several railroad lines met at Manassas, so there would be good transportation there for men and supplies. Much of the Confederate army was camped behind a stream called Bull Run.

The Confederate General Pierre Gustave Toutant Beauregard assumed that the Union army would strike at Manassas to take the railroad junction, and he had stationed most of his men between Bull Run and Manassas Junction. His left flank, to the west, was only thinly guarded. On July 21, McDowell's Union troops reached Bull Run. McDowell probed toward Manassas and discovered how strong the Confederates were there. He then sent a large force westward to cross Bull Run beyond the Confederate line. From there it could make a classic flanking maneuver, hitting the opposing army sideways, on its end. The Union troops outnumbered the Confederates by more than two to one and caught them by surprise. Nonetheless, the Confederates fought back fiercely. However, slowly they gave ground, retreating up Henry House Hill, a long open slope cut by some stone walls, at the top of which was the farm of the bedridden Judith Henry, who insisted on staying in the house during the battle and was killed by a shell.

By now General Beauregard was bringing in Confederate reinforcements to Henry House Hill from the main body of his troops in front of Manassas Junction. Among them was a regiment led by Thomas J. Jackson, a former professor at Virginia Military Institute. Jackson held his men firm just behind the crest of Henry House Hill. Another officer, seeing him sitting erect on his horse cried out to his men something like, "Look at Jackson standing there like a stone wall." Thus was born the legend of Stonewall Jackson, until his death by a mistaken shot from one of his own men, among the greatest of the Southern fighters in the Civil War.

Jackson's troops alone could not have won the battle. But now the forces on both sides were equal. For several hours the battle hung in the

Bull Run was actually a relatively small stream, however famous it became. Here it is shown with some battle debris scattered along the shore.

Much of the Battle of Bull Run swirled about Henry House Hill. Here are the remains of Henry House itself after it was destroyed by shells and fire.

balance. Two Union batteries of cannon were blasting away at the Confederate lines, causing much death and destruction. Suddenly they saw, coming out of the woods nearby, fresh troops in uniforms of blue, the Union color. Thinking they were Union reinforcements that were expected, the Northern troops held their fire. Suddenly the "reinforcements" opened fire on the artillery batteries from close range. The batteries were overtaken, and at that point the Union forces began to sag back. Beauregard sensed that he held the upper hand. He ordered a counterattack all along the line. Confederate troops charged forward, shouting the "yip yip yip" cry that became known as the rebel yell. The Union troops began to retreat. Soon the retreat turned into a run, and then into a panicked flight. Despite the efforts of the Union officers to hold the men in line, the soldiers continued to flee in disorganized panic the thirty miles back to the safety of Washington. They swarmed into the city, a broken army, many of them simply falling exhausted into the streets. In the first real battle of the war, the Union had suffered a devastating defeat.

It must be said that the confusion over the blue uniforms was not the sole cause of the Union defeat at the Battle of Bull Run: The panic of inexperienced troops was the main problem.

(But confusion over uniforms was common during the Civil War. At first, some Confederate soldiers, who had been in the United States Army before the war, still had the blue uniforms they had been issued, instead of the gray ones the Confederates wore. Later in the war, as cloth grew short in the South, many Confederate soldiers picked up pants, jackets, and shoes from Union corpses after a battle. Some ended up wearing a mix of Union, Confederate, and civilian clothing.)

The defeat at Bull Run might have been much worse for the North had Beauregard been able to follow up his victory with an attack on the disorganized and disheartened Union army, perhaps even taking Washington, and ending the war then and there. But his own troops were as disorganized and exhausted as the Union soldiers. Beauregard could do nothing further until he gave his troops a chance to lick their wounds. But the Confederacy had achieved at Bull Run what it wanted: to drive back the invading force. (Northern and Southern chroniclers of the Civil War sometimes use different names for battles. Southerners usually call this fight Manassas, while Northerners use the term Bull Run.)

The primary effect of Bull Run was psychological. Northerners were so disheartened by the defeat, and especially the panicked flight of Union troops, that some even concluded that the war was over. A few days later the *New York Tribune* advised Lincoln, "If it is best for the country and for mankind that we make peace with the rebels, and on their own terms, do not shrink from that."

In the South, however, there was nothing but pure joy, despite Beauregard's inability to chase the fleeing Union troops into Washington. Bull Run, so it seemed, showed that one rebel could indeed lick ten Yankees. The Confederates now believed that they would win, and it would take many battles and ten of thousands of rebel deaths to convince them otherwise.

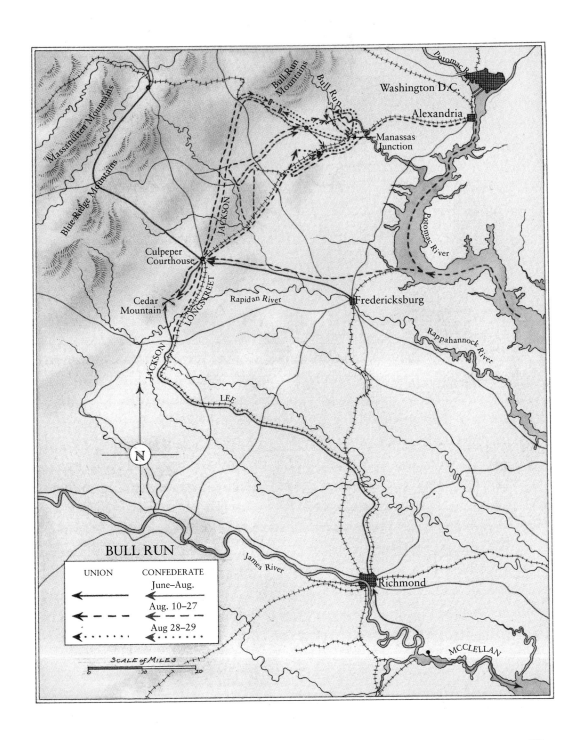

Potomac R.

Bull Run Mountains

Bull Run

Washington D.C.

Alexandria

Manassas Junction

Massanutten Mountains

Blue Ridge Mountains

JACKSON

Potomac River

Culpeper Courthouse

Cedar Mountain

JACKSON

LONGSTREET

Rapidan River

Fredericksburg

Rappahannock River

N

JACKSON

LEE

BULL RUN

UNION	CONFEDERATE
←	← June–Aug.
←---	←--- Aug. 10–27
←····	←···· Aug 28–29

James River

Richmond

MCCLELLAN

SCALE of MILES

0   10   20

CHAPTER III

A War to Free the Slaves

The Union defeat at Bull Run had discouraged many Northerners, but it had not disheartened Lincoln. He knew now that there would be no quick victory; but he was determined to fight on.

His first step was to bring in a new general to run the disorganized and dispirited Union troops in Washington. He chose General George B. McClellan, who had made a good record in the Mexican War fifteen years earlier. Lincoln's second step was to devise a strategy for a long war. McClellan in the east would attack Richmond. In the west another army would move into Tennessee, and cut the railroad line between Memphis and Richmond, thereby slicing an important Confederate supply line. At the same time attacks would be made up the Mississippi from the Gulf of Mexico, and down the Mississippi from Missouri. If the North could gain control of that great waterway, it could cut off the western states of the Confederacy—Texas and Arkansas, and most of Louisiana—from its eastern states. Slowly the Union forces began to ready themselves to attack the South from several directions at once.

The Union commander in the Mississippi area was General Henry W.

Halleck. Under him was a colonel named Ulysses S. Grant. Aged thirty-nine, Grant had known little but failure in his life. A West Point graduate, he had fought well in the Mexican War as lieutenant, but had later been thrown out of the army for drinking too much. He moved to Missouri, failed as a farmer, and was working as a clerk in a store when the Civil War broke out. Experienced officers were in demand, and Grant managed to rejoin the army as a colonel. His regiment was soon ordered into Missouri to fight a regiment of Confederates commanded by a Colonel David Harris. As Grant approached the Confederate position he was suddenly taken with fear, and almost backed off. He went on, however, and discovered the Confederate position abandoned. He said later, "It occurred to me at once that Harris had been as much afraid of me as I had been of him. This was a new view of the question I had never taken before; but it was one I never forgot afterwards."

Grant was promoted to brigadier general. He soon realized that the Tennessee and Cumberland Rivers, which ran roughly north to south and joined the Ohio just before its confluence with the Mississippi, were passageways into the South. The Confederates knew this, too, and had built forts along the river. Grant was given the job

Ulysses S. Grant, showing his strong, determined face. This portrait was painted after the Civil War, when Grant was president.

of capturing two of them, Fort Henry and Fort Donelson. Fort Henry on the Tennessee fell easily, but the Confederates had stationed twenty thousand men, under one of their ablest generals, Albert Sidney Johnston, at Fort Donelson on the Cumberland. Grant drew his troops up in a semicircle around the fort, which backed up against the river. The Confederates tried to fight their way out, but Grant, through brilliant generalship, forced them back after a bitter fight in a forest, and the Confederate garrison had to surrender. Tennessee's capital and major city, Nashville, was now open to Union attack, and was quickly taken. The Tennessee government was effectively out of the war, but it would take battles at Shiloh and Chattanooga to completely quell the rebellion there.

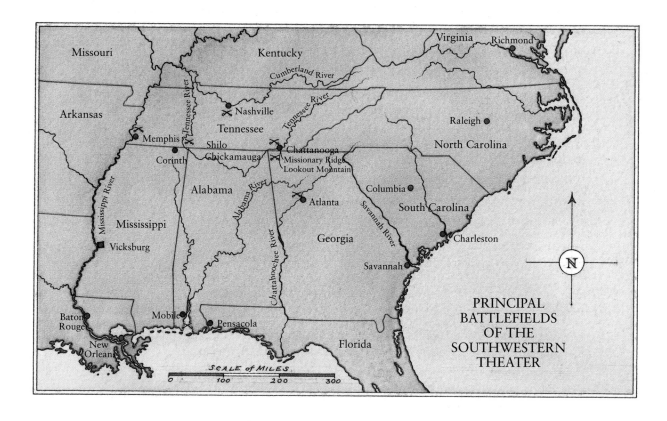

PRINCIPAL
BATTLEFIELDS
OF THE
SOUTHWESTERN
THEATER

The Confederate army was by no means finished. It retreated southward down to the little town of Corinth, in the northeast corner of Mississippi, just across the line from Tennessee. Grant went down the Tennessee River in pursuit, but was ordered by Halleck to hold up until additional forces arrived. Grant was waiting, near the small town of Shiloh, when the Confederates made a surprise attack, racing into Union camps at dawn and catching Federal soldiers with their weapons at rest, cooking breakfast.

The Union troops reeled back. As it happened, they were under the command of a general who would become almost as famous as Grant, William Tecumseh Sherman. Sherman managed to rally his troops and put together a defensive line on top of a small hill. Another general, Benjamin Prentiss, also managed to establish a defensive line in a patch of brush and trees, which Southern troops came to call soon "the Hornet's Nest." Although 18,000 Confederates attacked his 4,500 men, Prentiss refused to give in. His troops fired cannon into the charging Confederates at point-blank range. Still the rebels charged, coming across open ground like "maddened demons," as one Union soldier later put it. Finally, out of ammunition, Prentiss surrendered. But his courageous stand on that long day gave Grant time to reorganize his forces.

Grant now established a line not far from Shiloh. The Confederates pushed forward, taking ground. But Confederate troops were exhausted and hungry. The Confederate general, concluding that he had won, called off his men for the night, and wired Jefferson Davis that he had won a complete victory.

But he did not know Grant. Grant had seen much failure in his life, and it had made him less boastful than many of the other generals around him. One man who knew him said he was "the most modest, the most disinterested [minded] and the most honest man I ever knew, with a temper that nothing could disturb." But despite his modesty and lack of pretension, he had "an expression as if he had determined to drive his

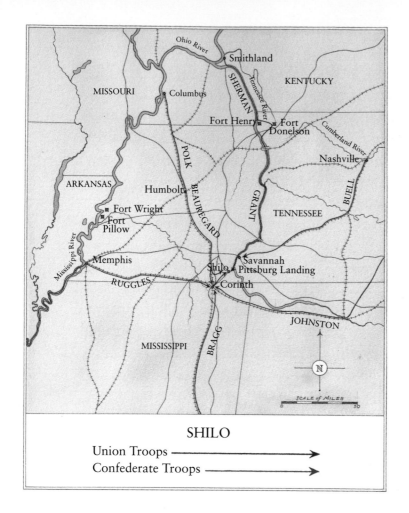

SHILO

Union Troops ──────────────→
Confederate Troops ──────────────→

head through a brick wall, and was about to do it."

That night at Shiloh, Grant knew that the long-expected reinforcements were arriving, and he determined to drive his head through that brick wall. Some of his officers, dismayed by losses of the day, urged Grant to retreat before the Confederates attacked again. Grant said, "Retreat? No. I propose to attack at daylight and whip them." Grant brought the reinforcements into line and in the morning counterattacked. The fighting grew ferocious. One Union soldier later wrote of passing through a field of dead and wounded during the fighting. "Their groans and cries were heart-rending. The gory corpses laying all about us, in every imaginable attitude, and slain by an inconceivable variety of wounds, were shocking to be-hold." A Confederate wrote, "I never realized the 'pomp and circumstance' of the thing called glorious war until I saw this . . . the dead . . . with their eyes wide open, the wounded begging piteously for help." General Sherman himself described "piles of dead soldiers' mangled bodies . . . without heads and legs . . . The scenes on this field would have cured anybody of war."

The Confederates were outnumbered, and as desperately as they fought, could not win. They pulled out of battle and withdrew southward. Grant gave chase briefly, but his own men were so exhausted he quickly gave up. It had been a great victory for the North, but causalities on both sides had been terrible—about 24,000 men killed or wounded in two days. (We should understand that the term "causalities" included dead, wounded, and missing, like those taken prisoner. About 14 percent of the Union wounded died; 18 percent of the Confederates.) Grant was criticized for nearly having lost the battle on the first day, and some people pressed Lincoln to remove him. Lincoln replied, "I can't spare this man; he fights." Ulysses S. Grant would be heard from again.

The Battle of Shiloh made it clear once and for all to both North and South that it was going to be a long and bloody war. Casualty lists were growing. The mood on both sides lost its exhilaration; it was still warlike, but now it was grim.

Back east the Confederate army was also finding itself a fighting general in Robert E. Lee. Lee and Grant, both West Point graduates who had served in the Mexican War, were in many ways opposites. Grant, fifteen years younger than Lee, was a bit roughhewn, a sloppy dresser and a drinker who did not care much about the formalities. Lee was unfailingly polite and dignified. When he sat erect on his famous horse, Traveler, he looked exactly like how a general ought to look. But the men were alike in that they were aggressive and liked to fight. They were both outstanding commanders. And just as Grant was seizing the initiative in the west, so Lee was about to seize it in the east.

Before we look at the eastern battles, we need to understand that the Civil War was, from the viewpoint of anyone studying it, a very disorderly affair. This was due to the overall strategy of both sides. Lincoln, under the tutelage of his generals, came to see that taking this or that city or piece of land did not much matter: The key to victory was to destroy the Confederate armies, cut off their supplies and kill their will to fight.

Just as the North found its general in Grant, so the South found its in Robert E. Lee, a man of impeccable bearing and command. Here he is seen on his famous horse, Traveler.

Union armies would thus not attack according to an overarching strategy, but would seek out the enemy and fight them wherever they were.

Conversely, because the strategy for the Confederacy was defensive, simply to hold off Union penetration of the South, it, too, would fight here and there as circumstances demanded. True, Lee would prove aggressive and would sometimes push into the North, as we shall shortly see. Lee wanted to bring the war to Northerners as they had brought it to the South; but he knew he could not really hold Northern territory. Lee would give the North a black eye, and then pull back.

As a consequence of these differing strategies, in the Civil War there was usually no established front line, no miles of troops drawn up in trenches and forts facing each other. Instead, until the final stages, the war was carried on by armies wandering around trying to find the enemy, or get away from him, as need be. Often battles occurred by accident, when armies happened to bump into each other.

After Shiloh, the next important battle began in the east, by accident. Stonewall Jackson took his troops up to Manassas, outside Washington, where he found great heaps of Northern supplies. His men ate their fill, packed up as much as they could carry, and burned the rest. Jackson then holed up on a wooded ridge not far from the old Bull Run battlefield. Here, on July 29, 1862, Northern troops stumbled on them. Fighting for several days, some of it over the old Henry House Hill field, was fierce, but in the end it was Union troops who fell back. Once again the North had suffered a severe defeat at Bull Run: The Confederates lost in killed, wounded, and missing 10,000 of 55,000 men (18 percent), the Union 16,000 of 65,000 (24.5 percent).

The Confederate army was again twenty miles from Washington. Northern troops were dispirited, indeed ashamed of themselves for having retreated back into the city. The voices of those ready to settle with the South grew stronger.

Abraham Lincoln, however, was resolute. Nonetheless, it was obvious that something had to be done to bolster Northern morale and inspire the troops to victory. And Lincoln finally came to believe that he must take a stronger stand against slavery.

It was a risky idea. The North had kept on its side the border states like Missouri, Maryland, and Kentucky, where there were plenty of slaveholders. Furthermore, many Northerners did not like blacks. Even Lincoln himself tried hard to keep the focus on the constitutional issue of secession. He had said all along that the war was to preserve the Union, not to abolish slavery or bring about any other great changes in American society.

But the majority of Northerners opposed slavery, and as the casualty lists got longer and longer, they became more and more determined that the war was not about union only but also freedom. Lincoln saw that if he made the war about slavery, as well as about preserving the Union, he might inspire the growing majority of antislavery Northerners to stick with the cause. In March 1862, he put forward a plan for "compensated emancipation," meaning that slaveholders would be paid for freeing their

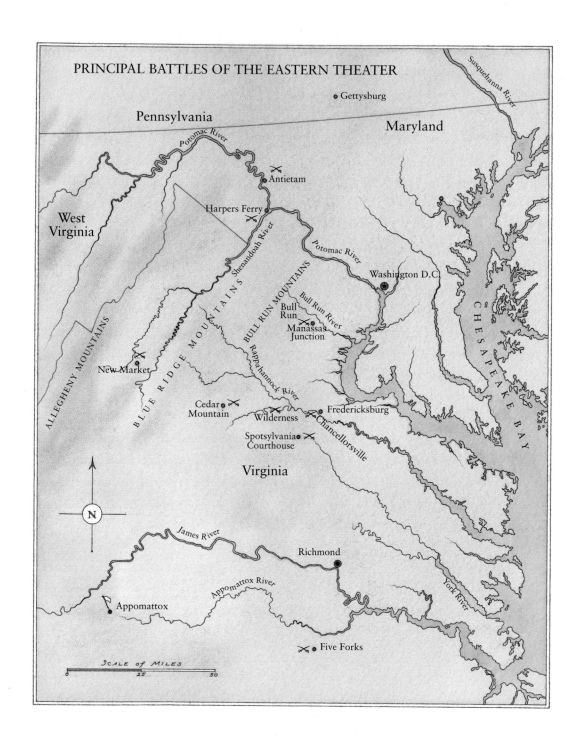

PRINCIPAL BATTLES OF THE EASTERN THEATER

Gettysburg

Pennsylvania

Maryland

Susquehanna River

Potomac River

Antietam

West Virginia

Harpers Ferry

Shenandoah River

Potomac River

Washington D.C.

Bull Run River

Bull Run

Manassas Junction

BLUE RIDGE MOUNTAINS

BULL RUN MOUNTAINS

ALLEGHENY MOUNTAINS

New Market

Rappahannock River

Cedar Mountain

Wilderness

Fredericksburg

Chancellorsville

Spotsylvania Courthouse

CHESAPEAKE BAY

Virginia

N

James River

Richmond

York River

Appomattox River

Appomattox

Five Forks

SCALE OF MILES

0   25   50

slaves. Lincoln reasoned that even though slavery existed mainly in the South, over the years the whole country had agreed to let it exist, and therefore the whole country could be asked to pay to get rid of it. Congress passed Lincoln's scheme, but of course it could not be forced on the South, and the border states ignored it.

Support for emancipation was growing, however. In July 1862, Congress, where a majority was ahead of Lincoln on the slavery issue, passed a law confiscating the property of rebels in territory taken by the North. As a result, tens of thousands of slaves were taken in as "contraband," that is, captured goods, and sent to work for the North building fortifications, tending the fields of captured plantations, and acting as personal servants to Union officers. Congress also decided to permit the Union to enlist black troops, if necessary. This measure was controversial: Many Northern soldiers did not like the idea of fighting side-by-side with blacks. Other people believed that blacks would not make good soldiers; yet others were afraid that if blacks were given guns they might turn them on whites. For the moment nothing was done about it.

Nonetheless, by the summer of 1862 Lincoln had become convinced that he must proclaim the emancipation of at least some of the slaves. He was aware that many officials in Europe, seeing the difficulty the North was having in subduing the South, were beginning to think they ought to come out in support of the Confederacy. An emancipation proclamation would commit antislavery Northerners more firmly to the struggle, and at the same time would make it clear to Europeans that a Northern victory would mean the end to slavery. But Lincoln was persuaded that it would not do to issue the proclamation on the heels of the Northern defeat at the Second Battle of Bull Run. It would seem like a desperation move. He must wait for a victory. And he depended upon General McClellan to get him one.

McClellan, we remember, had been brought in after the First Battle of Bull Run to pull together the disorganized forces in Washington. The

The American Civil War was of intense interest to much of the world, which wanted to see if the great democratic experiment would collapse. European newspapers sent correspondents to cover the action. Military people also wanted to see what new tactics and weapons might come out of the war. The group in this picture, wearing Union uniforms, includes the Duc de Chartres, the Prince de Joinville, and the Comte de Paris, all French nobility.

aging Winfield Scott was eased out. McClellan proved to be an astute and energetic organizer, and he quickly whipped the eastern army into shape. Unfortunately, McClellan was arrogant and considered Lincoln to be a country bumpkin. Equally unfortunate, he had a tendency to overestimate the strength of his opponents, and was constantly asking for more troops and more time to get ready. Earlier, the exasperated Lincoln had complained, "If General McClellan does not want to use the army I would like to *borrow* it."

But after the Second Battle of Bull Run, with Lincoln desperately in need of victory, McClellan was ready to fight. Lee, sitting outside Washington, knew he had not strength enough to try to take the city. He decided then to bring the war north into Pennsylvania and Maryland. A victory in Maryland might persuade Marylanders to come into the Confederacy. It might also encourage wavering European nations to support the South. Moreover, the Northern blockade was having an effect. In Northern cities and towns Lee would find wheat, milk, meat, clothing, and shoes that his men desperately needed—many of them were fighting barefoot.

Lee assumed that it would take McClellan weeks to restart his army after the Bull Run defeat. He decided to split his Confederate army, sending a division north to capture Harpers Ferry on the Potomac at the West Virginia border where Union troops were blocking his supply lines.

But McClellan fooled Lee. Within days he marched out of Washington with Union troops determined never again to run as they had. He headed toward Frederick, Maryland, about twenty-five miles west of Baltimore, looking for Lee. Lee, his forces split, retreated back into the Blue Ridge Mountains, waiting to see what happened at Harpers Ferry. Leaving some troops in the mountain passes to fight delaying actions, Lee brought the main body of his troops down into the area around the little town of Sharpsburg, between the Potomac River and Antietam Creek. Here he got news of a Confederate victory at Harpers Ferry, opening up his supply lines. He drew his troops up in front of Sharpsburg, and waited. McClellan fought his way through the passes in the Blue Ridge Mountains, and at 5:30 in the morning on September 17, he attacked Lee.

One historian has written: "The fighting at Antietam was among the hardest of the war. The [Union army] battled with grim determination to expunge the dishonor of previous defeats. Yankee soldiers were not impelled by fearless bravery or driven by iron discipline . . . Rather, they were motivated in the mass by the potential shame of another defeat."

According to this historian, sometimes in battle a frenzy overtakes the troops and produces a "sort of fighting madness in many men . . . This frenzy seems to have prevailed at Antietam on a greater scale than in any previous Civil War battle." One Union officer wrote many years later, "The men are loading and firing with demoniacal fury and shouting and laughing hysterically." By nightfall, 6,000 men were dead or dying, another 17,000 were wounded. Both sides had been badly mauled with Union forces getting the worst of it; but Lee had only 30,000 troops left, and he retreated into Virginia.

It is clear to war historians today that McClellan might have destroyed Lee's army at this point and ended the Civil War if he had thrown all of his troops into battle. Unfortunately, as ever, he believed that Lee had some huge number of troops in reserve, which was not the case, and he held back his own reserves. He might also have chased after Lee's exhausted troops as they fell back into Virginia, but he did not do that, either.

Nonetheless the Battle of Antietam, or Sharpsburg as Southern historians term it, was seen as a great victory for the North. It had cost the South much in men and supplies, it had ended the threat to Washington, and most important, had persuaded the English to stay out of the conflict for the moment. Northern spirits were greatly raised: Their soldiers had proved that they could fight with valor.

Lincoln now had the victory he had needed. Five days after Antietam he told his cabinet that he was going to issue the Emancipation Proclamation. He knew that it would offend the border states, but he felt they would not switch sides to join a Confederacy that it now appeared might be defeated. On January 1, 1863, all slaves in areas still in rebellion or owned by rebels still fighting, would be free. The Proclamation did not apply to the slaves in border states still within the Union or to parts of Louisiana and Tennessee controlled by loyal Unionists there.

At first glance it would appear that the Proclamation actually freed no slaves. But in fact thousands—probably tens of thousands—of slaves had fled their plantations and were living behind Union lines. These people would be freed by the Proclamation. Thousands more lived in areas still technically in rebellion but actually under Union control, like the Sea Islands on the coast of South Carolina. These, too, would be free.

One of the keys to Northern success at Antietam was the charge across the Burnside Bridge under heavy fire. During the Civil War, magazines, mostly in the North, sent artists to the battles to make quick sketches of the action, from which engravings would be made for use in the magazines. One of the best of these artists was Edwin Forbes, who made this sketch.

All battles end with scenes like this. Here are a few of the Confederate bodies left on the field after Antietam.

In addition, the Emancipation Proclamation had tremendous political and diplomatic significance. It made clear that the North was fighting not only to preserve the Union but to end slavery. This of itself made it difficult for European nations to come to the aid of the South, for to do so would only prolong the life of slavery. The Emancipation Proclamation also forced Northerners opposed to slavery to commit themselves to the war, for if they decided to quit, they would ensure that millions of blacks would live out their lives as slaves. On the other hand, many Northerners who enthusiastically supported a war to save the Union would not fight for black freedom. Scores of officers and men quit the army.

Thus the Emancipation Proclamation altered the Northern objectives of the war. No longer was it only a constitutional conflict over maintaining the Union. It was now a struggle to revolutionize Southern society and bring the ideals of liberty and equality proclaimed in the Declaration of Independence of 1776 to reality for the nation's four million slaves. Tens of thousands of them had already emancipated themselves by fleeing their plantations or just plain refusing to work where they were.

In elevating the war aims, Lincoln claimed he was freeing slaves strictly as a military necessity and was doing it in his capacity as commander in chief. But coupled with this legalistic justification was his statement that emancipation would be approved by "the considerate judgment of mankind and the gracious favor of Almighty God." Thus the Emancipation Proclamation held both legal and moral significance. In the Proclamation, Lincoln also invited black Americans to enlist in the armed forces. Writes one historian, "Here was revolution in earnest." Eventually over 190,000 African-Americans fought for the Union. Thirty-seven thousand of them died; certainly they believed that the war was about something more than the Union. As Hannah Johnson, until recently a slave, wrote Lincoln, "When you are dead and in Heaven, in a thousand years that action of yours will make the Angels sing your praises."

CHAPTER IV

A War at Home and at Sea

The Civil War had a profound effect not merely on the soldiers who fought in it but on nearly all Americans everywhere. Southerners particularly suffered from the ravages of shell and fire, as two great armies swept through cities, towns, and farmland in Virginia, Kentucky, Tennessee, Missouri, Georgia, and South Carolina. Pennsylvania and Maryland also saw fighting.

But the war reached out to touch Americans who lived hundreds of miles from the battlefields. Well over half a million families were devastated by the loss of a husband, son, or father. Another million had family members come home missing legs, arms, or parts of a face. About four million families spent months, or years, in anguish poring over casualty lists, praying they would not find the name of a son or husband. At least a third of American families had somebody in the armed forces during the war, which meant that virtually every American had a relative of some kind at risk. Almost everybody knew somebody who died in the war. In figures relative to the 1990s, it would be as though over five million American men died.

The war affected people at home in other ways, too. The armies gobbled up vast quantities of food, cloth, shoe leather, iron, timber—nearly everything America produced. The Union army alone needed a million and a half uniforms every year, along with three million pairs of shoe. As a consequence, nearly everything was in short supply. In the South, the switch from cotton to food growing made cotton scarce; Northern mill owners eventually found ways to get enough cotton to keep their mills running. But through the war the South was always short of cloth: As we have seen, many Southern soldiers had to pick up clothing from bodies on the battlefields.

Southerners particularly suffered from food shortages; millions of men had left their farms to fight and had to be fed by others. There were

occasional "bread riots" when civilian mobs, often composed of women incensed by high prices, smashed shop windows and took what they wanted. In Atlanta a gang of armed women went from shop to shop ordering the shopkeepers to lower their prices.

In the South there were almost constant shortages of food. Some shopkeepers took advantage of shortages to raise prices. In response women rioted, breaking into shops and taking the food they needed. Here is a newspaper illustration of such a food riot.

Because raw materials were being funneled into guns, bayonets, and army uniforms, manufacturers of civilian goods often could not get the material they needed. When the huge Northern textile industry, dependent on Southern cotton, was forced to shut down at the beginning of the war, most of its employees were thrown out of work, and some went hungry. The families of soldiers also suffered. The farm of a man who had gone to war had to be worked by his wife and children. Wives of factory workers in the army often went into the factories themselves, leaving their children to run loose in the streets. In Hartford, Connecticut, in one wartime year, of 359 charity cases, 233 were the families of soldiers.

Though few women faced the war firsthand, the war affected them nonetheless. In the nineteenth century it was not considered proper for women to become doctors or lawyers, or work at certain kinds of jobs thought of as "men's work." With the wartime shortage of labor, women were needed; very quickly they began to take over certain formerly all-male jobs, as nurses, clerks in offices, and as farm laborers. (In time some of these occupations, such as nursing, came to be seen as strictly female work.)

Neither army was particularly well set up to deal with the hordes of wounded the war produced, or the much larger numbers of men who came down with serious illnesses: The death rate from diseases like cholera and dysentery was far higher than deaths from battle. Often, due to the scarcity of ambulances, doctors, and stretcher bearers, men groaning in pain from serious wounds lay for hours, or even days, on the battlefield. Inevitably many died who might have been saved with quick attention.

Confederate women were the first to come to the aid of the wounded because the war was fought on their home grounds, where the wounded were among them. Southern women volunteered as nurses, or even started small hospitals for sick soldiers. In the North women were chiefly responsible for putting together an organization called the United States Sanitary Commission, inspired by the work of the celebrated English-

A Northern army hospital, probably near Washington, D.C. Many army hospitals near battle sites were much rougher than this. The picture was taken by the famous Mathew Brady, whose Civil War photographs are among the best. The camera was still in an early stage of development; the Civil War was the first war to be extensively photographed, and showed what photography could do.

woman Florence Nightingale, who had nursed British soldiers during a war against Russia a few years earlier. The "Sanitary," as it was called, trained nurses, sent inspectors out to teach soldiers how to take better care of their health, and supplied nurses for military hospitals. A great many people were shocked by the idea of respectable women going into army hospitals, where they were exposed to sights and language few of them had known before. But the nurses were popular with the soldiers and the "Sanitary" performed great services in saving the lives of the sick and wounded.

While most of the sick and wounded were treated near the battlefield, many of them were sent to hospitals near their homes. Women worked as nurses in these hospitals, too. One of them, Sarah Woolsey, wrote about "an awful boy with no arms, who swears so frightfully (all the time he isn't screeching for currant pie or fried meat, or some other indigestible) that he turns you blue as you listen." But most female nurses stuck it out and performed nobly.

Perhaps the most famous of these nurses was Clara Barton, a tiny woman who was dogged, even ferocious, in driving through her ideas. In July 1862, she managed to persuade the surgeon general of the Northern armies to let her go into army camps after battles to aid the sick and wounded. She did great work in getting medical supplies to the men. After the war she was instrumental in establishing the American branch of the Red Cross.

Millions of women also gathered to roll bandages, knit stockings, and put together Christmas packages for soldiers. Some even made visits to their fathers, sons, and husbands at the front, particularly to care for them when they had been wounded. The family of Captain Fiske, wounded at Fredericksburg, tended him near the battlefield until he died. The Civil War thus helped to show that women could do a lot of jobs they had not been allowed to take previously, especially in the caring professions, and as clerks in offices and shops.

Clara Barton was important in organizing nursing programs for the Northern armies. Small but dynamic, she went on to start the American branch of the Red Cross.

American civilians on both sides were deeply affected by the war. Here a group of Southern women near Cedar Mountain in the Shenandoah Mountains, where a famous battle was fought, roll bandages for wounded men.

The war had political effects, too. For one thing, as the war ground on, it became clear that the army could not be filled by volunteers alone. Both sides established drafts, conscripting men whether they liked it or not. The drafts were extremely unpopular. Indeed, in the South many people felt that the draft was the sort of tyranny they thought they were fighting against, and disappeared into the forests. But large numbers of men were drafted anyway.

Probably the most controversial of political actions during the war was Lincoln's decision to suspend the right to a writ of habeas corpus. The term means "have the body." If somebody is arrested, he can ask for a writ of habeas corpus from a judge. Then the government must show that it has some good, legal reason for arresting the person. Habeas corpus was put into the Constitution to keep governments from arresting people without a legal cause.

However, the Constitution says that habeas corpus can be suspended during a "rebellion or invasion." Shortly after Fort Sumter Abraham Lincoln suspended habeas corpus so he could arrest people who were suspected of being disloyal to the Union. Lincoln also said that those arrested could be tried in military courts, which had stricter rules. During the war some fourteen thousand people were arrested under Lincoln's order.

Many people denounced Lincoln for suspending habeas corpus, claiming that he was making himself into a dictator. Such a radical action, critics said, should only be taken by Congress. But Lincoln pointed out that the Constitution does not say who is permitted to suspend habeas corpus, only that the government can do it. He had a sworn duty to "preserve, protect, and defend the Constitution," and he must do what was needed to keep his oath.

Jefferson Davis, too, suspended habeas corpus in the Confederacy, and made a point of getting approval from the Confederate Congress. Nonetheless, he too came under much criticism. One citizen of Richmond said the edict would bring a "reign of terror." But the *Richmond Enquirer* spoke for most people when it said, "Our business now is to whip our enemies and save our homes. War, of course, never respects civil rights; indeed individual rights are often among the first casualties. We can attend to questions of theory afterwards."

The Civil War, thus, was "fought" at home as well as on the battlefield. It has been called the first "total" war. It may not have been as "total" as World War II, when bombers carried death directly to unarmed civilians, but it did draw into it one way or another, especially by suffering the loss of a loved father or son, more American civilians than any war since.

The war was also fought on the sea. So much attention has been given to the famous land battles, like Gettysburg and Bull Run, that we often forget how important the sea war was. While the Union could not have won the war by sea power alone, its ability to interfere with Southern shipping was critical to victory.

When the Civil War broke out, navies of the world were in a period of great changes. Steamboats had proven practical early in the 1800s, and navies were beginning to equip their warships with steam engines, although they usually had sails as well for use when the wind was good. But this movement was only beginning, and at the start of the war most of the Union navy consisted of wooden sailing ships. Half of them were in disrepair and out of commission at the time, anyway.

The Confederacy was in worse condition. It had never had its own navy, and its merchant fleet was small. Moreover, it did not have the seafaring tradition of the North, New England in particular, and thus had few trained seamen.

Both sides immediately began reequipping merchant ships for war duty, building new ones, and buying others from France, England, and elsewhere. The North wanted ships mainly to throw its blockade around Southern ports; the South wanted ships to break the blockade. The Confederate government commissioned merchant ships as privateers—that is to say, legal pirates who could capture Northern ships. Jefferson Davis also ordered the building of fast blockade-runners—slim steamships with low profiles, painted gray and burning hard coal, which gave off less telltale smoke than the soft coal usually used.

But the North had the advantage in its already existing fleet, and its large shipbuiding industry. Step-by-step it closed off Southern ports. Particularly important was the taking of much of the Sea Islands that run down the coasts of the Carolinas and Georgia. From here they could keep a watch out for Southern blockade-runners.

The Confederacy eventually managed to buy and equip in England some large warships, like the Alabama, which roved the seas and picked off Northern shipping, but there were far too few of them to do much harm.

While the blockade was undoubtedly the most significant part of the naval war, the sea war was critical to the battle for the Mississippi, too. As we have seen, the North was eager to get control of the Mississippi, which would cut off the western states of the Confederacy. Grant had successfully driven the Confederates out of Tennessee, giving the North control of the river north of Vicksburg, Mississippi. The idea now was for Grant to take Vicksburg, although that proved not to be easy.

Meanwhile the Union navy would launch an attack on New Orleans, near the Mississippi's mouth. In late April 1862, a huge Union fleet under Admiral David Glasgow Farragut slipped into the mouth of the Mississippi, a hundred miles below New Orleans. The mouth of the river was guarded by forts on both banks. The Confederates had run a boom across the river to block the way, and had scattered mines in the water, called torpedoes in those days. For two days Farragut's fleet bombarded the forts with cannon from the ships, but the Confederates held firm. Finally Farragut decided to take a desperate gamble. He had himself lashed to a mast where he could get a good view of things, and ordered the ships to charge the boom. Somebody mentioned the torpedoes in the water. "Damn the torpedoes," Farragut shouted, "full speed ahead." The ships crashed over the boom and safely through the mines, and Farragut's cry became a slogan for the North. The forts were now cut off from their supply base in New Orleans. Farragut proceeded up the river and bombarded the defenseless city. It surrendered on April 26, and was occupied by General Benjamin Butler, a man who became notorious by his rough treatment of the citizens of New Orleans. Although the Confederates still held a stretch of the river between

Admiral David Farragut was the hero of the capture of New Orleans by the North. He drove his ships through a minefield to race past the guns guarding the city, crying, "Damn the torpedoes, full speed ahead."

New Orleans and Vicksburg, the South had lost one of its major ports.

The most famous naval battle of the Civil War had much less strategic importance, but its long-range effects were enormous. Shipboard cannon had been growing in power and by the 1850s a well-aimed shot would penetrate the wooden hulls of fighting vessels. In the 1850s the French and the English built a few experimental ships with heavy iron plate covering the wooden hulls. Americans started their own experiments as the war broke out. At the time, one of the Union navy's biggest ships, the *Merrimack*, was laid up for repairs in the Norfolk, Virginia, navy yard. The Confederates seized it, and began to convert it to an ironclad vessel. They ripped off much of the upper part, and built on top of it a barnlike structure made of pine and oak two feet thick, over which was laid iron sheeting two inches thick. Inside of this fortress were ranged ten cannons. It was renamed the *Virginia*.

News of such a strange construction could not be kept secret. The Union quickly began to build an ironclad ship of its own. This one had an equally novel design—a flat hull low in the water, on top of which was placed a turret with only two cannons, but which could be revolved to shoot in any direction. The ship was called the *Monitor*.

Neither the *Monitor* nor the *Merrimack* (now the *Virginia*) could maneuver quickly, and because they sat low in the water they could not be used in the open sea where waves in a storm might swamp them. Additionally both were slow. But they would be impervious to enemy fire; or so it was thought.

The *Virginia* was first into the water. It immediately sank two of the Union navy's wooden warships and drove another one aground with hardly any damage to itself. The North was thrown into a panic. Fortunately for Northerners, the *Monitor* was now ready and heading south. On March 9, 1862, the two ships met in the first-ever battle anywhere between ironclad vessels. For hours they banged away at each other, but the shells bounced harmlessly off the metal plating. Finally the

Sailors on the deck of the famous Monitor, *which fought in the first battle of ironclad ships. The gun turret in back revolved to allow the cannons to shoot in any direction.*

Virginia gave up and retired up a river. The *Monitor* did not follow, and the battle was over. They never fought again—neither side wanted to risk its great weapon.

But the lesson was learned: The future belonged to warships of iron run by steam. In a moment, the navies of the world had been made obsolete. Both the Union and the Confederacy continued to build ironclads of differing designs; but the revolving turret proved most effective and is employed on warships today.

In the end, it was the old story: The North had the machines and the material; the South was short of everything. Never was the Confederacy able to build a navy large enough to really challenge the Union. Day after day the Union drew the noose of the blockade tighter. Still, the North could not win by sea power alone. Sooner or later it had to invade the South, destroy its armies, and break its will to fight. The critical battles would be fought on land.

CHAPTER V

The Tide of the Battle Turns

Despite the Union advantage at sea, in 1863, when the war was two years old, the Confederacy remained triumphant on land. The Union had had its victories at Antietam, New Orleans, and Shiloh, but the South had had great triumphs twice at Bull Run and elsewhere. It had kept the invaders out of most of the South, had preserved its capital at Richmond, and had twice come close to taking the Union's capital.

In May 1863, the South had yet another victory, at the little town of Chancellorsville, Virginia, where Lee repelled a Northern attempt to encircle his forces and force them into open combat. The defeat at Chancellorsville filled the North with despair. When Lincoln heard the news he turned "ashen," and said, "My God! What will the country say?" Some Northerners began demanding that Lincoln bring an end to the war. But that Lincoln would never do. And he was finally about to be rewarded in the west.

A year earlier Farragut's gunboats had taken New Orleans. Grant had been working his way down the Mississippi, and much of the river was now in Union hands. But the South still held Vicksburg, Mississippi, on the east bank of the river, keeping the connection between the eastern and western Confederacy open. The city was the key to the river. It was heavily fortified, and the South believed it could not be taken.

Farragut, in another daring attack, now ran his gunboats up the Mississippi past the Confederate cannons at Vicksburg, giving Grant naval forces to go with his army. Through the winter of 1862-63 Grant tried several times to march his men through the bayous and swamps in the approaches to Vicksburg from the north, but made little progress. He then decided on a daring plan. He would transport his army across to the western side of the Mississippi, slip downriver there until he was well below Vicksburg, where he could attack it from the south. Meanwhile, the gunboats would once again crash past Vicksburg, along with some transport ships to carry the troops across the river. It was a risky scheme, for Confederate guns in Vicksburg might sink his ships and his army then would be stuck on the west bank of the river.

On the night of April 16, 1863, the little fleet charged down the river. In Vicksburg Confederate soldiers started fires along the riverbank to light up the river so gunners in the city could see the boats churning past. Vicksburg's gunners fired 525 shells at the ships and made sixty-eight hits, but all except one of the boats got through. The first part of Grant's plan had succeeded.

He now marched his troops down the west bank of the Mississippi. When he was well below Vicksburg he ordered his favorite general, William Tecumseh Sherman, to feint an attack north of the city. While the defenders were distracted, Grant slipped his army across to the east side of the river.

He could now have attacked Vicksburg from the south. However, he knew that less than fifty miles farther east, in the state capital, Jackson, another Confederate army was gathering. This force could attack him from the flank while he was marching on Vicksburg. Once again he took the bold approach. He marched toward Jackson, living off the countryside,

An artist's idea of the Northern fleet charging past Vicksburg under cannon fire. The defenders pushed burning rafts into the path of the ships, one of which can be seen at left.

and in a series of brilliant tactics, beat the Confederates again and again. He then caught some of the force defending Vicksburg out in the open, defeated it in yet another bloody battle, and drove it back into the city.

But the Confederates were not yet finished. Vicksburg, they believed, was impregnable. And indeed it nearly was. On May 19 Grant ordered a direct assault on the defenders. The Confederates were deeply entrenched and threw Grant's men back. A few days later Grant tried again, and again was thrown back. Grant settled in to besiege the city.

The defenders begged the Confederate command for help. Why could not an army be sent to hit Grant from the rear? But the Confederate officers in charge replied that there were no troops to spare. There was, really, no hope. Vicksburg held out through June, as the people ate rats, then dogs and cats. Finally, with the defending soldiers too sick and starving to fight in any case, the city surrendered. The date, ominously for the South, was the Fourth of July. Very quickly Grant took the remaining Confederate strong points below Vicksburg, and the Confederacy was split in half. Grant's Vicksburg campaign, Lincoln said, was "one of the most brilliant in the world," and many historians agree. Lincoln went on to say, "Grant is my man and I am his for the rest of the war."

One of the smaller battles in the Vicksburg campaign was a stand made by black troops at Milliken's Bend—not very important from a military standpoint, but of considerable psychological significance. From the beginning of the war free blacks in the North had offered to serve in the army. They were always turned down. Partly this was because the Union government knew that the use of black troops would inflame Southerners and inspire them to fight harder. But mostly it had to do with racial prejudice: Many Northern whites felt that it would lower them to fight alongside African-Americans, and besides, it was believed that former slaves and even free blacks would not make good fighters, despite the fact that thousands had fought effectively in the American Revolution and other earlier wars.

But gradually opinion in the North changed, as the need for men grew. The Emancipation Proclamation authorized the organization of some African-American regiments, and some black troops were thus at Milliken's Bend in the Vicksburg campaign, where they fought with bravery. One white officer of black troops there wrote from the battlefield that his outfit of six hundred men, five hundred of them blacks, had been attacked by about 2,500 Texans. "I never felt more grieved and sick at heart than when I saw how my brave soldiers had been slaughtered . . . I never more wish to hear the expression, 'the niggers won't fight.' Come within 100 yards from where I sit, and I can show you the wounds that cover the bodies of sixteen as brave, loyal and patriotic soldiers as ever drew a bead on a Rebel." African-American troops were driven by the knowledge that they were fighting not only for the freedom of their fel-

At first the North discouraged black men from volunteering for the army, fearing that they would not have the courage to fight. Eventually, however, black troops were admitted, forming their own units, usually with white officers. They proved valiant in battle; many of them died fighting for the end of slavery.

lows in the South, but to prove to the world that blacks could die as bravely as whites. Their fortitude in battle began to change opinion, at least in the North. "Public sentiment has undergone a great change in the past month or two," wrote one black soldier from Philadelphia, "and more especially since the brilliant exploits of several colored regiments."

Black soldiers, too, had grown in confidence. One sent a written message to the woman who held his daughter in bondage: "My child is my own . . . you may hold onto her as long as you can but . . . the longer you keep my child from me the longer you will have to burn in hell and the quicker you'll get there . . . I have no fears about getting Mary out of your hands. The whole government gives chear (sic) to me and you cannot help yourself."

Meanwhile, back east, Robert E. Lee was once again looking for a way to bring the war to the enemy. He decided to march his army north into Pennsylvania and smack hard at the Union army. He hoped to accomplish several things. For one, he would get his troops into rich Pennsylvania farmland and out of war-ravaged Virginia, where there was little enough left for civilians to eat, much less a huge army. For another, if he could achieve a victory—and he was sure he could—he might bring wavering England in on the Southern side. Finally, one more Union defeat might discourage Northerners enough to sue for peace.

After the great Confederate victories at Second Bull Run and Chancellorsville, Lee had concluded that almost any body of Southern troops could defeat any number of Northern troops. He said, "There never were such men in an army before. They will go anywhere and do anything if properly led." Lee's overconfidence would prove costly.

Lee now began to move his troops into Pennsylvania—a major invasion of Northern soil. The Union force in the east was put under the command of General George Gordon Meade, who had a good combat record. Meade went looking for Lee's troops.

One of Lee's main objectives was to capture supplies from the well-stocked North. One of his generals heard that there was a storehouse filled with shoes in the little town of Gettysburg, Pennsylvania, near the Maryland border, southwest of Harrisburg, the state capital. He headed his troops for Gettysburg.

At about the same time, a Northern general noticed that a number of roads from various directions met at Gettysburg. The town had strategic value, and he moved his troops in, and stationed them on high ground northwest of the town. Suddenly he saw Confederate troops approaching and ordered his troops to fire on them. The startled Confederates attacked, and thus, almost by chance, began the most important battle of the Civil War.

Neither Lee nor Meade had intended to fight at Gettysburg, but events were out of their control. The generals engaged in the first fighting sent messengers scurrying with requests for help. Very quickly units

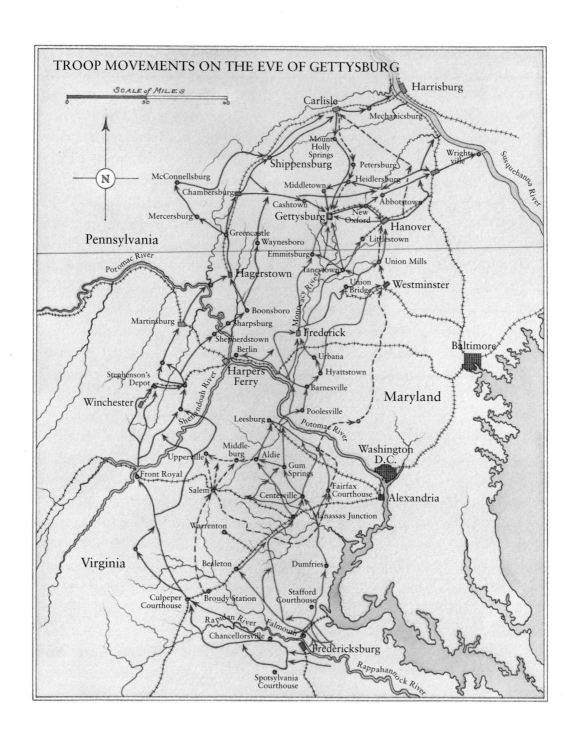

TROOP MOVEMENTS ON THE EVE OF GETTYSBURG

SCALE of MILES

Harrisburg

Carlisle

Mechanicsburg

Mount
Holly
Springs

Shippensburg

Petersburg

Wrights-
ville

McConnellsburg

Chambersburg

Middletown

Heidlersburg

Susquehanna River

Mercersburg

Cashtown

Abbotstown

Pennsylvania

Gettysburg

New
Oxford

Greencastle

Hanover

Waynesboro

Littlestown

Potomac River

Emmitsburg

Union Mills

Hagerstown

Taneytown

Westminster

Union
Bridge

Boonsboro

Baltimore

Martinsburg

Sharpsburg

Frederick

Shepherdstown

Berlin

Urbana

Stephenson's
Depot

Harpers
Ferry

Hyattstown

Winchester

Barnesville

Maryland

Leesburg

Poolesville

Potomac River

Middle-
burg

Aldie

Upperville

Gum
Springs

Washington
D.C.

Front Royal

Salem

Fairfax
Courthouse

Centerville

Alexandria

Manassas Junction

Warrenton

Virginia

Bealeton

Dumfries

Stafford
Courthouse

Culpeper
Courthouse

Broady Station

Rapidan River

Falmouth

Chancellorsville

Fredericksburg

Rappahannock River

Spotsylvania
Courthouse

from both sides began to gather in and around Gettysburg, and by mid-afternoon 24,000 Confederates and 19,000 Union troops were facing each other northwest of the village. At this moment Lee himself arrived. Typically, he quickly ordered an attack. The Confederates charged, shouting the rebel yell. They drove the Union troops back to a low hill south of town, called Cemetery Ridge. It was a good position to defend, and here the Northern troops dug in. More troops continued to gather, until there were 160,000 soldiers at Gettysburg.

Lee, emboldened by his early success in the battle, and convinced that his men were unbeatable, decided on a frontal attack. One of his subordinates, General James Longstreet, put up an argument: The Union position on the ridge was too strong. But Lee was adamant: His brave men had beaten the Yankees again and again, and they would do so at Gettysburg. He ordered Longstreet to attack the next day, July 2, 1863.

At the south end of Cemetery Ridge were two rocky knobs, which stuck up above the ridge, called Big Round Top and Little Round Top. If the rebels could take one of these high points, they could bring up cannon and fire along the Union line into Union trenches. As it happened, Meade had concentrated his forces on the other end of the line, where he believed Lee's forces were strongest. Little Round Top was virtually undefended. At 4:00 in the afternoon, just as Longstreet's men were about to charge, a Northern general noticed that there were few Union troops on the Little Round Top. He ordered a Northern brigade to run up Little Round Top on the double. They got there just in time to take on the charging Confederates. For two hours they fought. Particularly hard pressed was the Twentieth Maine. After two hours the Maine regiment was out of ammunition, and a third of its men were down. Their commander ordered them to fix bayonets on their empty rifles. With a yell they charged downhill into the startled Confederates, who were exhausted after so much vicious fighting. Many of the rebels surrendered and the rest fled. Little Round Top was saved for the North.

The view from Little Round Top at Gettysburg, as Longstreet's corps, seen in the distance, moved up to attack. The defeat of Longstreet's charge was crucial in the Northern victory at Gettysburg. This sketch was made on the spot by the famous war artist, Edwin Forbes.

This kind of fighting at close quarters went on all up and down the line. Particularly hard fighting took place in a peach orchard and wheat field in front of the southern half of Cemetery Ridge. Just as at Little Round Top, the Confederate troops almost broke through the Northern line in several places; indeed, twice the rebels actually got a foothold on top of the ridge, only to be thrown back by determined Northern fighters. At nightfall the Yankees were still on Cemetery Ridge. Between them, the two sides had lost 35,000 men dead and wounded in less than two days of fighting. Man met bullet at the rate of about thirty a minute; every two seconds someone got hit.

But General Lee believed he had nearly broken through Northern lines several times. One more push might do it. On the morning of July 3 General Longstreet once again begged Lee to give up direct assaults, and try to maneuver around the Union left. Lee refused, and ordered Longstreet to attack with three divisions of 15,000 men. Longstreet said

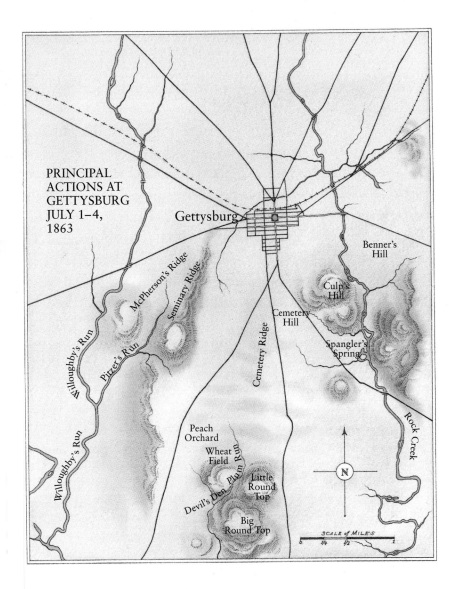

PRINCIPAL
ACTIONS AT
GETTYSBURG
JULY 1–4,
1863

Gettysburg

Benner's Hill

Culp's Hill

Cemetery Hill

Spangler's Spring

McPherson's Ridge

Seminary Ridge

Willoughby's Run

Pitzer's Run

Cemetery Ridge

Rock Creek

Peach Orchard

Wheat Field

Plum Run

Devil's Den

Little Round Top

Big Round Top

N

SCALE of MILES

later that he told Lee, "General Lee, there never was a body of 15,000 men who could make that attack successfully."

Heavyhearted, Longstreet ordered a massive bombardment of Cemetery Ridge. The Union cannons answered, and then fell silent, put out of action by Confederate shells—or so Longstreet thought. He ordered the attack, with the Confederate troops spread out over a mile-long front. Among them were fresh troops commanded by General

George Pickett. The rebels swept forward, and suddenly the Union cannons began to bark; they had not been destroyed, but had stopped firing to decoy the Confederate troops. The rebels fell like mowed wheat, but still on they came. Pickett's men took the worst of it. Yet some of them made it over a stone wall at a place on Cemetery Ridge called the Angle. Desperate Union reinforcements drove them back. The rebels began to stream back down Cemetery Ridge, across the open ground they had charged over, now filled with the bodies of the dead and groaning wounded, to the safety of the trees on the other side of the field. The Battle of Gettysburg was over. Half of the 15,000 attackers had been killed or wounded in that terrible half hour. General Lee went among his

A Southern sharpshooter lies dead in a trench at Gettysburg, one of the thousands of men who lost their lives in the battle.

men consoling them, and telling them that it was his own fault. Shortly he began a retreat back into Virginia.

Later on, Meade was criticized for not having immediately counter-attacked. If he had, he might have destroyed Lee's army, and ended the war then and there. At the time he believed that Lee was still too strong, and he did not want to ruin his own army by doing what Lee had just done—attack a strong defensive position. The Union had already lost a quarter of the men at Gettysburg—23,000 soldiers; the Confederates had lost a third of theirs, 28,000.

Gettysburg was seen as a great victory for the North: The seemingly unbeatable Lee had been beaten. As one New Yorker wrote, "The charm of Robert Lee's invincibility is broken." Antiwar Northerners were silenced and the French and British, who had once been seriously considering coming in to support the Confederacy, now backed off for good. Although nobody knew it at the time, when Pickett's courageous men had climbed over that stone wall at the Angle on July 3, the Confederacy had reached high tide. Gone forever was the possibility of a Southern advance into Northern territory. The next day came the news that Grant had taken Vicksburg. "Though the war was destined to continue for almost two more bloody years, " writes one historian, "Gettysburg and Vicksburg proved to have been its crucial turning point." Southerners fell into despair, and Lee offered to resign. Though millions of Southerners were still ready to fight, the cause of the Confederacy was becoming desperate.

Lincoln decided to make the most of it. As was frequently the practice, men who had died at Gettysburg were buried at the battlefield, creating a vast new cemetery. Lincoln did not usually visit such cemeteries, but in order to point up the importance of the victory, he went to Gettysburg for the dedication ceremonies. Thus, on November 19, 1863, he made at Gettysburg the most famous speech ever made by an American. It was very short: It can be recited in less than two minutes. But it was remarkable for what it said.

Nowhere in the speech did Lincoln condemn the South for anything; nowhere did he boast of the great Northern victory at Gettysburg. He made just a few simple points. Once again he made it clear that both the preservation of the Union and the freedom of the slaves were equally critical. In the Declaration of Independence, said Lincoln, "our fathers brought forth . . . a new nation conceived in Liberty, and dedicated to the proposition that all men are created equal.

"Now we are engaged in a great civil war, testing whether that nation or any nation so conceived can long endure." The buried soldiers shall not have died in vain if the war gives the American people "a new birth of freedom" so that "government of the people, by the people, and for the people, shall not perish from the earth." Lincoln twice made allusions to slavery. In the first sentence, "conceived in *liberty*, and dedicated to the proposition that all men are created *equal*" alludes to slavery. And in the last sentences the phrase, "that this nation, under God, shall have *a new birth of freedom*" was again an allusion to slavery.

In the Gettysburg Address, then, Lincoln was putting the world on notice that the great war was about preserving the Union *and* ending slavery. "We shout for joy," wrote the great black leader Frederick Douglass, "that we live to record this righteous decree." The Emancipation Proclamation had freed *some* of the slaves. Now Lincoln was saying that the war would go on to free *all* of them. It was also clear that the minds of the people of the North had been changed, too. They had endured years of suffering. The bloody carcasses of their sons, brothers, fathers, and husbands were a sacrifice too great to go unrewarded. They wanted something for their pain. It all had to be worth something, and they would end slavery as the price of their suffering. And Southern society would be revolutionized.

CHAPTER VI

Sherman Marches to the Sea

The South's position after the losses at Vicksburg and Gettysburg was bad, even desperate, but defeat was not inevitable. There was still the chance that if Lee could hang on and inflict enough casualties on Union soldiers, Northerners in time might grow weary of the war and consent to some sort of negotiations, although it is hard to imagine Lincoln or his people accepting either an independent Confederacy or the continuation of slavery. But if his generals did not win some important battles, some other man more inclined to compromise these issues might win the looming presidential election of 1864.

Although most Civil War battles were fought at close quarters, often in woods and marshes, some still took place in open fields with massed troops facing each other in traditional European style. Grant had come to understand that the old system of warfare, where massed armies charged one another on open ground, would no longer work. Americans had learned the value of building strong defensive positions by throwing up earthwork barricades and digging trenches. Furthermore, step-by-step, guns were being made more deadly. Rifling—spiral grooves on the inside of gun barrels that made bullets fly more accurately—was made universal in all new guns issued to the troops. The old ball-shaped bullet was replaced by the *minié* bullet, cylindrical with a pointed nose as bullets are today, which made them even more accurate. Finally, toward the end of the war, the Union armies got newly invented repeating rifles, which could fire seven shots without reloading. A soldier behind an

Prior to the Civil War, most wars were fought by armies maneuvering on open ground. With the advent of newer, more deadly weapons, the generals gradually learned that defenders holed up in well-fortified trenches, tunnels, and man-made caves, where they would be safe from shells, could hold off a much larger force. Typical of such defenses are these bombproof shelters constructed near the end of the war at Fort Sedgwick, near Petersburg, where Lee made his last stand.

earthworks barricade equipped with these improved rifles was deadly against an enemy charging over open ground. It was calculated that you needed three attackers to match one defending soldier.

Grant had come to understand that the frontal assault had become very costly in men. Attacks across open fields, like Pickett's nearly suicidal charge at Gettysburg, showed that. The way to win the war, Grant realized, was to destroy the South's ability to fight by cutting off its food, clothing, weapons, shoes. This was after all the basis of Scott and Lincoln's Anaconda plan at the beginning of the war. Although clever work by Southern supply officers kept the Confederate troops armed right to the end, by the time of Gettysburg many rebel soldiers were barefoot, dressed in rags, and often hungry. Grant was determined to make matters for them worse.

His first move was to send troops eastward toward Chattanooga, Tennessee. The city was an important railroad junction, the door into Georgia and the Southern heartland. It was, however, located, in rough mountain territory cut by ravines and gorges. Initially the Confederates had the upper hand, and in September 1863 bottled up the Union troops in Chattanooga. In November Grant brought fresh troops to the rescue. The Confederate commander, General Braxton Bragg, held Lookout Mountain, rising steeply out of the plain south of the city, and a low hill to the east called Missionary Ridge. These heights commanded the city and would have to be taken by Federal troops. Grant sent his men into battle. They drove up the steep flanks of Lookout Mountain through a patchy fog and with surprisingly few losses, forced the Confederates down the other side.

The attack on Missionary Ridge was not so easy. Grant's troops hit at both ends of the ridge and were driven back. Grant had reserve troops commanded by General George H. Thomas. These troops had made a brave stand at Chickamauga a few weeks earlier, but in the end had been driven back into Chattanooga. Now Grant sent them forward to drive at

This is Missionary Ridge in a shot taken after the Battle of Lookout Mountain. General Thomas's troops attacked up the hill at right, and gained a surprising victory.

the center of Missionary Ridge. This was a tough assignment, for the Confederates had had plenty of time to dig three parallel trenches along the slopes of the ridge. But Thomas's men, unhappy about having been driven back into Chattanooga in the earlier fighting, had something to prove.

Grant and Thomas stood at a command post a mile to the rear where they could see the action on the slopes of the ridge. As they watched, they saw the Union troops sweep into the first of the three lines of trenches. Then, a few of them leaped out of the trenches and raced farther uphill toward the second line of trenches. More followed, and then more and more, until the whole line was rushing upward.

Grant was alarmed, for he did not want to lose the whole force in a heedless attack on a strong defense. "Thomas," he said angrily, "Who ordered those men up on the ridge?" Thomas replied, "I did not." In fact, it was the soldiers themselves who had taken the initiative. They realized that they could easily be fired upon in the trench by Confederates farther up the ridge. And they wanted to show the Confederates their worth as fighters. So on they rushed. The astonished Confederates could not believe what they were seeing, these bluecoats charging "completely and frantically drunk with excitement, " as someone later said. Shouting derisively, "Chickamauga, Chickamauga," they raced forward. The Confederates broke and ran, and by nightfall Missionary Ridge was in Union hands. So was Chattanooga, the door to Georgia. Later on someone remarked to Grant that the Southern generals had considered Missionary Ridge impregnable. Grant replied with a smile, "It *was* impregnable."

Lincoln was now even more certain that Grant was his man. In March 1864 the president called Grant to Washington, and put him in charge of all Northern forces. It was the first time they had met—the gangling president and the slightly scruffy general. They were both men who had seen hard times in their lives, both realists who knew what they could expect from other people and what they could not. They respected each other, and together were determined to win the war.

Grant immediately ordered an invasion of Georgia. Now began one of the great epics of the war, General Sherman's March to the Sea from Chattanooga, into Georgia, and then through Atlanta to Savannah. Like his chief, William Tecumseh Sherman

The dashing General William Tecumseh Sherman, with the characteristic determined look on his face.

wore a rough beard and a rumpled uniform. But he was a more talkative, outgoing man who liked to enjoy himself. He did not intend to enjoy himself on his new assignment, however. His orders from Grant were not so much to take territory but to inflict "all the damage you can against their war resources." Later many Southerners would condemn Sherman for burning their crops, taking their horses and mules, and leaving desolation behind. But that was exactly the point—to make sure that

Sherman deliberately laid waste to the land through which he marched, in order to deprive the South of the food and supplies it needed, to bring Southerners to their knees. The strategy was successful. This picture shows Columbia, the capital of South Carolina, after Sherman marched through. Hardly a building remains standing in the area.

Southerners did not have food for their soldiers, and to show them they could not win. Sherman's men had orders not to hurt civilians, and generally they didn't, although it was bound to happen sometimes. Nonetheless, even today many Southerners feel that Sherman's army had been needlessly cruel.

At first Sherman was faced by a good Southern general, "Old Joe" Johnston. "Old Joe" knew that his troops were outnumbered, and he fought a number of bloody delaying actions, holding Sherman back by clever maneuvers. Sherman was also skilled at maneuvers, however, and worked his way to the Chattahoochee River, near Atlanta. Jefferson Davis wanted Sherman not merely delayed but thrown back, and he replaced Johnston with General John B. Hood, a more aggressive fighter. Hood began attacking, using up his strength, and on September 1 the Confederates gave up Atlanta. Sherman then proceeded to take everything he could carry and burned a great deal of what was left.

Sherman now decided that rather than go after Hood's army, he could do more by marching through the undefended territory between Atlanta and Savannah about 250 miles to the southeast on the sea, once again destroying crops and barns, and taking horses, mules, and cattle. He had trouble persuading Grant and Lincoln to agree, but finally they did. Faced by only a tiny Confederate force, Sherman worked his way unobstructed from Atlanta to Savannah, laying waste to the countryside. On December 10 he offered Savannah to Lincoln as an early Christmas present. The Confederacy had earlier been split on a line north and south by the Union conquest of the Mississippi. Now it was split on a line east and west from Chattanooga to Savannah.

For the North, Sherman's victories through the summer and fall of 1864 could not have come at a better time—it was an election year. Today it seems incredible, but Lincoln feared that he might not be reelected. The war in Virginia had not been going well for Grant, as we shall shortly see. Many Northerners had never favored the war, and even those who had at first been enthusiastic about bringing the South to heel had become disheartened by the deaths of young men they had known in their towns and villages, and the sight of others trying to rebuild their lives around a missing arm or leg. In just two months, May and June, Union forces had suffered over 44,000 casualties. By mid-summer of 1864, many Northerners were ready for a president who would negotiate a peace with the South. In August Lincoln made a note, "It seems exceedingly probable that this administration will not be reelected."

Then, in September, Sherman took Atlanta. On October 17 he started from Atlanta to the sea. He deliberately cut his communications with his commanders so they could not order him to withdraw; but Northerners could get Southern newspapers, and they followed the story of Sherman's triumphant march to Savannah. Northern hopes that they could win the war after all began to rise, and Lincoln was reelected. The war would continue.

CHAPTER VII

The Slaughter Finally Ends

In the summer of 1864, while Sherman was making his famous march through Georgia, back in Virginia Grant and Lee were engaged in a series of ferocious battles that each hoped would bring a final victory. It was now clear to everybody that the Confederates could not bring the war into the North as they had tried to do at Gettysburg. Lee's idea was simply to keep his army intact, inflict casualties on Northern armies in hopes that Northerners would finally sicken of the slaughter and force Lincoln—or a new president—to start negotiations. As much as Lee liked to attack, he recognized that he could best preserve his army by staying on the defensive.

Grant understood all of this. With the North's much larger population he had a two-to-one manpower advantage. His scheme was to force Lee to fight, luring him out into the open where the Union's manpower advantage would count.

In May, about the time that Sherman was starting his march through Georgia, the two great armies met in a series of battles in an area known as the Wilderness, about twenty miles west of Fredericksburg, Virginia.

The Wilderness was a heavily wooded area filled with a tangled thicket of underbrush—not a very good place for a large force of men to attack through. For the first two days, the battle seesawed back and forth. Everything was in confusion. Gunsmoke filled the woods, making it difficult to tell friend from enemy. Cannons set fire to the underbrush, so that many wounded men burned to death before their comrades could drag them to safety. Both sides kept maneuvering to outflank each other; both sides took severe losses, but Grant, constantly attacking, lost more than twice as many as Lee.

Despite his losses, Grant pushed Lee a couple of miles back to a town called Spottsylvania. Here the Confederates hastily threw up long dirt breastworks to form a defensive line shaped like a rough V. Immediately Grant began throwing troops at this strong defensive position. Initially

In the Battle of the Wilderness the underbrush caught fire from the heavy shelling. Here Northern soldiers carry a wounded comrade away from the flames, while other wounded on the ground beg for help.

he had some success: Union troops broke through Confederate defenses, and might have taken the whole position, but reinforcements failed to come up in time.

Two days later Grant, encouraged by his near success, ordered another massive attack. There followed some of the roughest fighting of the war. Once again the Union broke through, only to be thrown back by a fierce counterattack that Lee tried to lead himself until his own men ordered him back to safety. Now Grant ordered a large force to hit at the point of the V, which would become known as "the Bloody Angle." For eighteen hours the two armies fought at close range with bullet and bayonet. One veteran of the fight recalled, "The flags of both armies waved at the same moment over the same breastworks, while beneath them Federal and Confederate endeavored to drive home the bayonet through the [gaps] in the logs." One historian wrote, "Impelled by a sort of frenzy, soldiers on both side leaped on the parapet and fired down at the enemy troops with bayoneted rifles handed up from comrades . . . Blood flowed as copiously as the rain, turning trench floors into a slimy ooze where dead and wounded were trampled down by men fighting for their lives." In those two days at Spottsylvania twenty thousand men were killed or wounded. These were among the bloodiest days of the war.

Despite his losses, Grant was determined to keep pressure on Lee. He said, "I'm going to fight it out on this line if it takes all summer." There was more bloody fighting, especially at Cold Harbor, not far from Richmond—perhaps Grant's worst defeat, with seven thousand casualties in a few hours. In the end Lee was able to slip his forces into the town of Petersburg, which controlled communications into Richmond from the south. Grant tried attacking Petersburg, but soon realized that frontal assaults only ground his army down. He settled in to besiege Petersburg.

Meanwhile, in the Shenandoah Valley to the west, a fine farming country that was critical to the Southern food supply, other armies were fighting for control. Fighting here, too, was fierce, but finally the Union troops, under one of their best generals, Philip Sheridan, drove the Confederates out and stripped the Shenandoah of its vital food supplies.

By the winter of 1864-65, with Lincoln reelected by a margin of 400,000 votes—many of them from soldiers in the field and on leave at home—the North was clearly winning the war. The Mississippi, the Shenandoah Valley, and Georgia were under Union control. Lee was holed up in Petersburg, while Grant sat outside, like a cat watching a mouse hole. Yet Grant could not strike the knockout blow.

Through the winter and into the spring, the two armies sparred lightly, and waited. Inside Petersburg, food grew scarcer and scarcer. Lee knew that he would have to break out fairly soon in order to feed his troops. If he got loose perhaps he could find a way to join up with remnants of other Confederate armies and form a defensive line somewhere to the south.

Then, at the end of March, Grant sent General Sheridan to attack Lee's right flank at a place called Five Forks, west of Petersburg. If Sheridan could win, he would cut an important railroad line into Petersburg. He could also close off any chance for Lee to escape to the west. On April 1 Sheridan overran the Confederate defenses at Five Forks. Lee now had no choice, and on the night of April 2, he slipped his troops out of Petersburg, and began scrambling westward, hoping to get clear of Grant's troops and then turn south, to meet with other confederate troops in North Carolina. But Grant was south of Lee, and he kept moving with him. Lee could not make the turn. For nearly a hundred miles they marched and fought, marched and fought, and still Lee could not get far enough ahead of the Union forces to permit him to turn south.

On April 7, at the little town of Appomattox Court House, Lee found Grant blocking his way not only south, but west, too. On April 8 Lee sent his cavalry out in a last desperate attempt to fight his way out of the trap. The Southern cavalry charged into Sheridan's mounted troops at a place called Bent Creek, and pushed through. But very quickly Union reinforcements were brought up. The Confederate cavalry, hungry, exhausted, and greatly outnumbered—like the rest of Lee's army—was forced to fall back. That was Lee's last gasp. "There is nothing left for me to do," the defeated general told his staff, "but to go and see General Grant, and I would rather die a thousand deaths."

They met on April 9 in the home of a man named Wilmer McLean in the village of Appomattox Court House. The terms of surrender were quite simple: Lee's men would not be taken prisoner, but would be allowed to go home, to plow their fields and plant their crops. Those who had claims to a horse or a mule could take them. Meanwhile, Grant would feed the starving Southern soldiers from his plentiful stores. It was, everyone believed, a time for healing, not revenge. There were still other Confederate troops farther south; but with the surrender of Lee's army the South was effectively finished, and soon the other troops surrendered.

The McLean House, where Grant and Lee met to discuss the terms of Lee's surrender, ending the terrible Civil War.

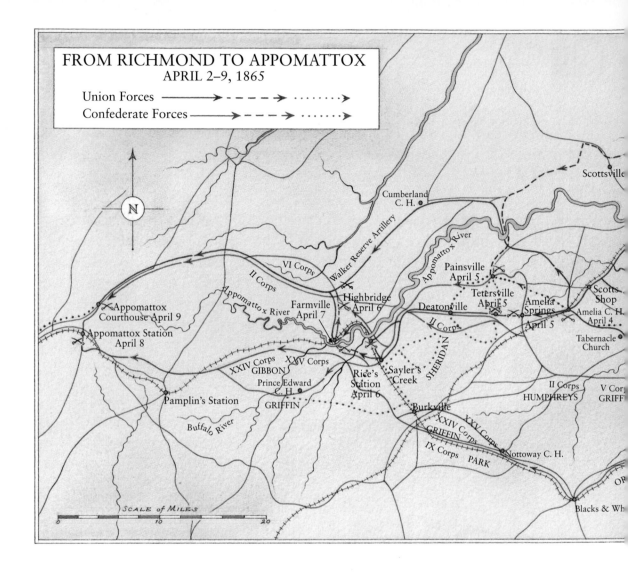

FROM RICHMOND TO APPOMATTOX
APRIL 2–9, 1865

Union Forces ——————➤ – – – – ➤ ⋯⋯⋯➤
Confederate Forces ——————➤ – – – – ➤ ⋯⋯⋯➤

Scottsville

Cumberland
C. H.

Walker Reserve Artillery

Appomattox River

VI Corps

II Corps

Painsville
April 5

Scotts
Shop

Highbridge
April 6

Tettersville
April 5

Amelia
Springs
April 5

Amelia C. H.
April 4

Farmville
April 7

Deatonville

Appomattox
Courthouse April 9

Appomattox River

Appomattox
Station
April 8

II Corps

Tabernacle
Church

SHERIDAN

XXIV Corps
GIBBON

XXV Corps

Rice's
Station
April 6

Sayler's
Creek

Prince Edward
C. H.

II Corps
HUMPHREYS

V Corps
GRIFFIN

Pamplin's Station

GRIFFIN

Burkville

XXIV Corps
GRIFFIN

XXV Corps
PARK

Buffalo River

IX Corps

Nottoway C. H.

OR

Blacks & Wh

SCALE of MILES
0   10   20

Was there any way the Confederacy could have won the war? Large
strategic and political decisions, of course, played a part in the outcome.
If Lee had kept to his defensive strategy and refrained from invading the
North; if he instead of Grant and Sherman had grasped the concept of
"total war" first; if Davis had been able to inspire and strengthen the will
of the Southern people the way Lincoln had the Northerners; . . . And, as
always in war, there were dozens of "critical moments" when things
might have gone the other way. If the Confederate troops had managed

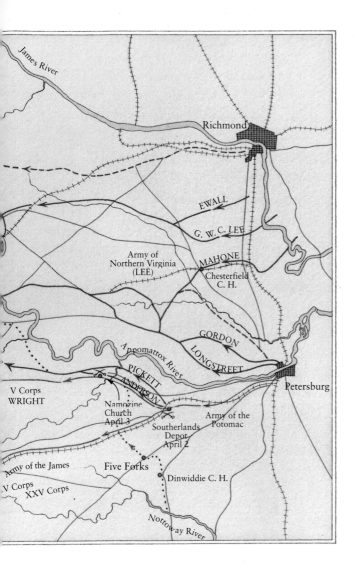

to hang on at Cemetery Ridge at Gettysburg, if they had attacked Grant from the rear at Vicksburg, if they had not broken and run at Lookout Mountain, perhaps the South could have found a way to win. But on the other hand, if Meade had followed up the victory at Gettysburg with an attack on Lee's retreating troops, or if McClellan had been more decisive early in the war and had taken Richmond, the North might have won much sooner. There are always ifs: Things happen or don't happen and the course of the war flows this way and that.

But the North won because it could—it had the will and the resources to do the job, and the intelligence to see how it could be done. In Lincoln the North had a leader who had the will, and would not give in, no matter how long the casualty lists grew. Lincoln also recognized that Ulysses S. Grant was a man as dogged and determined as he was. And both came to realize that with the North's larger population and much greater industrial might, they could wear the South down. This they did, by tightening the blockade, producing enough victories to keep England and France from supporting the Confederacy, taking the Mississippi and cutting off supplies from the west, ravaging the Shenandoah Valley and

The price of war. Northern troops bombarded Richmond, Virginia, the Confederate capital, ferociously throughout the war. They were unable to take it until the end, but they left it in ruins. Here two women in black clothes, signifying that they are in mourning for their dead, walk through a landscape of rubble.

Georgia, and hammering away at Lee until he could no longer fight. The strategy was terribly costly in human life: indeed it was this unanticipated and increasingly immense loss of life and limb that turned a war to save the Union into a war to free the slaves, as well. The Union had "won" despite the deaths of so many men and boys. This was the price they had to pay to continue the democratic experiment and end slavery for millions of blacks.

The South could have won only if Northerners, discouraged by the casualty lists, lost heart. But once Lincoln, with the Emancipation Proclamation and the Gettysburg Address, had committed the North to ending slavery—something millions of Northerners had taken for granted all along—most Northerners agreed that to give up without obtaining that goal would condemn them forever as moral cowards. Lincoln, for one, would not do that, and neither would millions of the ordinary people who would have to pay the price.

The war's end left much of the South in ruins, with hundreds of thousands of farm animals killed, "absolute destitution" along Sherman's route, and the Shenandoah Valley "almost a desert." The plantation economy was desolated, buildings were in shambles, and the great majority of people were impoverished. But worst, of course, was the death of nearly 260,000 Southern men—over one-fifth of the adult white male population of the seceded states. Thousands of Southern soldiers returned to their devastated farms, themselves devastated—without arms and legs, broken in health and spirit, earning for their sacrifices only poverty and premature death.

Thirty-seven thousand African-Americans lost their lives fighting for their freedom. But those alive were free at last. Their lives under the threat of the lash and the disruption of their families was over. For them, at least, the carnage was worth the results. And for white Americans, too, making the slaves free freed everyone, for democracy cannot survive in a house divided.

BIBLIOGRAPHY

For Teachers:

Berlin, Ira, Barbara J. Fields, Steven Miller, Joseph P. Reidy, eds. *Free at Last: A Documentary History of Slavery, Freedom, and the Civil War*. New York: New Products Development, 1992.

Boritt, Gabor S., ed., et al. *Why the Civil War Came*. New York: Oxford University Press, 1996.

Cornish, Dudley Taylor. *The Sable Arm: Black Troops in the Union Army, 1861–1865*. Lawrence: University Press of Kansas, 1987.

Current, Richard N. *The Lincoln Nobody Knows*. New York: Hill & Wang, 1958.

Davis, William C. *Rebels and Yankees: The Fighting Men of the Civil War*. New York: W. H. Smith, 1989.

Donald, David H. *Lincoln*. New York: Simon & Schuster, 1995.

Doughty, Robert, et al. *The Civil War: The Emergence of Total Warfare*. Lexington, Mass.: D. C. Heath, 1996.

Griffith, Paddy. *Battle Tactics of the Civil War*. New Haven: Yale University Press, 1989.

McPherson, James M. *Battle Cry of Freedom: The Civil War Era*. New York: Oxford University Press, 1988.

Time-Life Books, editors of.*Echoes of Glory*. New York: Time-Life, 1991.

Wills, Garry. *Lincoln at Gettysburg: The Words That Remade America*. New York: Simon & Schuster, 1992.

For Students:

Bolotin, Norman, and Angela Herb. *For Home and Country: A Civil War Scrapbook*. New York: Lodestar Books, 1995.

Catton, Bruce. *The Civil War*. New York: American Heritage, 1971.

Damon, Duane. *When This Cruel War Is Over: The Civil War Home Front*. Minneapolis: Lerner, 1996.

Davis, William C. *Rebels and Yankees: Fighting Men of the Civil War*. New York: W. H. Smith, 1989.

Hansen, Joyce. *Between Two Fires: Black Soldiers and the Civil War*. New York: Franklin Watts, 1993.

Kent, Zachary. *The Civil War: A House Divided.* Springfield, NJ: Enslow, 1994.

Kirchberger, Joe H. *The Civil War and Reconstruction: An Eyewitness History.* New York: Facts on File, 1991.

Marrin, Albert. *Unconditional Surrender: U. S. Grant and the Civil War.* New York: Atheneum, 1994.

Meltzer, Milton., ed. *Voices from the Civil War: A Documentary History of the Great American Conflict.* New York: Thomas Y. Crowell, 1989.

Mettger, Zak. *Till Victory Is Won: Black Soldiers in the Civil War.* New York: Lodestar Books, 1994.

Smith, Carter. *The First Battles: A Sourcebook on the Civil War.* Brookfield, CT: Millbrook Press, 1993.

Steins, Richard. *The Nation Divides: The Civil War, 1820–1880.* New York: Twenty-First Century Books, 1995.

Time-Life Books, editors of. *Echoes of Glory.* New York: Time-Life, 1991.

Time-Life Books, editors of. *Soldier Life (Voices of the Civil War).* New York: Time-Life, 1996.

INDEX

JAMES LINCOLN COLLIER is the author of a number of books both for adults and for young people, including the social history *The Rise of Selfishness in America*. He is also noted for his biographies and historical studies in the field of jazz. Together with his brother, Christopher Collier, he has written a series of award-winning historical novels for children widely used in schools, including the Newbery Honor classic, *My Brother Sam Is Dead*. A graduate of Hamilton College, he lives with his wife in New York City.

CHRISTOPHER COLLIER grew up in Fairfield County, Connecticut and attended public schools there. He graduated from Clark University in Worcester, Massachusetts and earned M.A. and Ph.D. degrees at Columbia University in New York City. After service in the Army and teaching in secondary schools for several years, Mr. Collier began teaching college in 1961. He is now Professor of History at the University of Connecticut and Connecticut State Historian. Mr. Collier has published many scholarly and popular books and articles about Connecticut and American history. With his brother, James, he is the author of nine historical novels for young adults, the best known of which is *My Brother Sam Is Dead*. He lives with his wife Bonnie, a librarian, in Orange, Connecticut.

DATE DUE

MAY 1 8 2005

JAN 0 2 2007

APR 1 6 2008

PRINTED IN U.S.A.

GAYLORD